PREACHING AT THE PARISH COMMUNION
ASB EPISTLES—SUNDAYS: YEAR ONE

PREACHING AT THE PARISH COMMUNION

ASB Epistles—Sundays: Year One

R. O. OSBORNE

MOWBRAY
LONDON & OXFORD

ISBN 0 264 66903 7

First published 1984
by A. R. Mowbray & Co. Ltd
Saint Thomas House, Becket Street,
Oxford, OX1 1SJ

Typeset by Set Fair Limited
Printed in Great Britain by The Thetford Press Ltd, Thetford, Norfolk

FOREWORD

If you are looking for the Word of God spoken or written by one who knows the people of God as well, then this book of sermon outlines is for you.

Robin Osborne has served in rural and urban parishes for many years, latterly at St Mary's Cheshunt, and now at St Mary's Penzance. Although he has a well stocked mind he is far from bookish; though his sermons are substantial they are never dull; and, though he is as diligent and disciplined a priest as any you could meet, he has a sure understanding of frail humanity and laughs both joyfully with other people and delightfully at himself.

As are his interests, so is his religion, thoroughly Catholic. But his loyalties are marvellously English and Anglican. Read on and discover how. You will pray all the better for the experience.

+ PETER TRURON:
Lis Escop, Truro 1983

CONTENTS

vii

NINTH SUNDAY BEFORE CHRISTMAS

All perfection found in Christ

Colossians 1.15–20 (JB)

1 *A wider vision*

One of the tourist attractions of this church, ever popular, is going up the tower: school parties, all of us on Ascension Day, many young urchins who ring the doorbell at a time when all good Vicars should be asleep; all enjoy it.

You have been up yourselves, so you know how the spiral staircase leads you upwards, ever upwards. And you know how the little slit windows, if they are not silted up with seagulls' nests, reveal views of earth and sea below.

As you climb upwards, ever upwards, you realize that the views you get from these little windows, and eventually from the ringing chamber itself, become wider ever wider. At first all you can see is the odd gravestone. A further twist of the stair and another window, and an angle of path appears, and a corner of church roof. Yet another twist, and you are above the rooftops with a view of the Vicarage hydrangeas. Out onto the roof, and the whole panorama is laid out before you: what had been odd views and unconnected scenes now fall into a pattern. Paths and roads lead here and there, buildings reveal their plans, the horizon stretches from the Lizard to Penlee Point.

This is my parable for this first Sunday in the Church's year. Today we begin another cycle in the Church's cycle of seasons. Round and round we go, year by year, through Advent to Christmas, through Epiphany to Lent, through Holy Week to Easter, through Ascensiontide to Pentecost, and back along the green straight to the starting post again. To the unimaginative this is a treadmill, where you keep walking but get nowhere, like the donkey in Carisbrooke castle. But there is all the

1

difference between a treadmill, on which you get no-where, and a spiral staircase, where every turn of the stair brings you a higher and fresher vision, a more expansive view, and eventually a view of heaven or Tesco's warehouse (you must allow any analogy to break down somewhere!).

2 *All the glory of God*

I would remind you of that strange encounter which Moses had with God when he demanded to see the Lord. And the reply came that he would not see the face of God, but that all God's glory would be made to pass before him. The faithful Christian, going steadily about his work and worship through the Christian year, does indeed experience the Glory of God passing before him. There is simply too much of God to begin to comprehend in one view. But season by season, festival by festival, we are presented first with this and then with that aspect of the majesty and holiness and glory of God—his humility at Christmas, his sacrificial love on Good Friday, the joy of his presence at Easter, his royal majesty at Ascension-tide, the fullness of the Spirit at Pentecost. Each is true all the time, and is there all the time. It is only our vision which is limited.

To the faithful Christian each round, each year, is like a twist in the spiral staircase. As he matures in wisdom and understanding, so does his view become more compre-hensive. Isolated facts about God merge, as he climbs higher, into a pattern. His grasp of the truth becomes less fragmented and more of a whole. He himself becomes less divided and more integrated. Only when you finally climb out onto the top of the tower does everything fall into place. I think perhaps in my parable that had better stand for the final vision of God, and of all things in God.

Be faithful. Keep climbing. Certainty and understand-ing will follow as surely as day follows night. Wholeness is what we crave. And have you noticed that what we always used to read as 'righteousness' is translated in our new

Bible by 'integrity'? We become more integrated, more consistent, more whole.

3 *Christ is all in all*

Let me in this new year (because it is not a repetition, but a new season offering fresh opportunities, fresh vision), let me apply this wider vision particularly to our understanding of Jesus.

At the beginning of our pilgrimage, so limited is our childish grasp of history, Jesus barely stands out against the background of wonder-workers, magicians, heroes, against which we live our childish lives. As we mature, the sheer attractiveness of Jesus catches our imagination: we come to love him as our friend; we give him our allegiance as our Lord. At some other stage we come to recognize him in this sacrament: from tripping so lightly to the altar with thoughts scattering here, there and everywhere we begin to approach with awe, with reverence, encountering a holiness from which the very angels guard their eyes.

As in climbing the tower, where we do not lose our first visions but come to see them as part of a greater whole, so we never lose the sense of Jesus as brother and friend, but this takes its place in a deeper knowledge of him as holy Lord. And while we retain this personal knowledge of him we gain the wider vision still, of the Cosmic Christ:

> *Christ is the image of the unseen God and the first-born of all creation, for in him were created all things in heaven and on earth: everything visible and everything invisible.*

EIGHTH SUNDAY BEFORE CHRISTMAS

Why did Cain murder him?

1 John 3.9–18 (TEV)

1 *Under the power of death*

You may remember the series of aircraft crashes in the 1950s which involved the Comet airliners, and how the painstaking reconstruction of the wrecks, and the testing of a full-scale model to the point of destruction, eventually led to the explanation. It was an explanation so simple that even we could understand it: that of 'metal fatigue'.

It is, after all, a principle known to every small boy who creases paper before he tears it, and to every man who determines the break in a sheet of glass by the direction of a small scratch on its surface. It is a principle known to every student of geology, how along the weak points below the earth's surface immense forces wait to erupt. It was my privilege to know one of the scientists who did so much to solve the problem of those disappearing aircraft; it is the experience of every human being, and no privilege at all, to know the eruptions of hatred, violence and evil, which occur along the cracks and faults of human nature, along those lines which are the petty boundaries we draw and define to separate what is ours from what is not.

It is as if, just as beneath this crust of earth on which we are floating at this moment there are immense pressures and instabilities ready to assert themselves along any geological fault or weakness, so beneath our human society, which at the best of times is in uneasy equilibrium, there are immense pressures and instabilities ready to assert themselves. And the faults and weaknesses can be quite tiny, like the first scratch in your pane of glass or sheet of metal. How many family quarrels can be traced back to something so trivial that under normal circumstances it would not be noticed? Just as a ladder runs out

4

of control through a stocking (you must tell me if my illustrations are out of date!) so do these little scratches run out of control through society when given the chance: one shot at Sarajevo precipitated the first World War; a racist yields such power because what he implies about race links up with that little fear of the unknown which is in each of us. What is 'confrontation' but an illustration of the same truth, that a line of emotional demarcation has been allowed to fester into a line of battle.

2 *Do not be surprised if the world hate you*

These divisions are not always tiny and insignificant. They may run along the great emotional frontiers: that between white skins and black skins; that between exuberant youth and crabbed old age; that between Catholic and Protestant in Northern Ireland. It is along these faults that the great primeval urges of mankind seize their chance, and produce at best tension and at worst hatred and destruction. It is our duty to remember those luckless people who have lived, and still live, along these lines of weakness in our society, who become victims of forces quite beyond their control—forces which well to the surface when weak men and wicked men, with an instinct born of hell itself, touch that line of self-concern or that line of fear or that line of greed, which spreads to tear society apart. The eruption recedes to leave in its wake men and women wounded in body and mind, or dead.

> *So do not be surprised, my brothers, if the people of the world hate you . . . Whoever does not love is still under the power of death. Whoever hates his brother is a murderer.*

3 *True love, which shows itself in action*

Christians above all can face that basic human need when faced with distress or despair or bereavement—the need actually to *do* something.

As eucharistic men and women we make present here, in the space and time which we inhabit, something which is eternally true. At that deepest of all chasms which have faced mankind, his separation from the loving purpose of his heavenly Father, the sacrifice of Christ brings healing and unity.

> *This is how we know what love is: Christ gave his life for us. We too, then, ought to give our lives for our brothers : If a rich person sees his brother in need, yet closes his heart against his brother, how can he claim that he loves God?*

We are the rich persons, for we are the children of God.

> *My children, our love should not be just words and talk; it must be true love, which shows itself in action.*

SEVENTH SUNDAY BEFORE CHRISTMAS

Chosen people

Romans 4.13–end (JB)

1 *Abraham and his descendants*

That's a funny thing for Jesus to say: 'Before Abraham was born, I am.' It is one of his great 'I AMs'—I am the Good Shepherd, I am the Bread of Life, I am the Vine, and so on. But of them all this is the most startling, if you put yourself in the place of those who first heard it. Abraham was the great father of God's people, and he lived thousands of years before Jesus. Indeed, when you are ploughing through the Old Testament, that enormous part of the Bible which tells of the preparation for the coming of Jesus, it is with Abraham that you enter real history. So you Cubs and Brownies will know that whatever Jesus meant by saying 'Before Abraham was born, I am', it was obviously a claim to be someone much greater than Abraham; and we shall come back to that in a moment.

The point is that Abraham was chosen by God, so let's think about 'choosing'. We spend our lives making choices about many things, if only whether to have bacon-flavoured crisps or shrimp-cocktail flavoured crisps! In a few days' time, as November comes to an end, the organist and I will catch each other's eye, and say, 'Yes, well, I suppose we must'. And then we will sit down and choose the hymns and music for December. We do it together so that, if anyone complains, each of us can say it was someone else's choice. And I say, 'There's a third Sunday coming up—let's choose hymns that the Cubs and Brownies know.' Sometimes it is people we have to choose. Countries choose their leaders. I have been out of touch, in every sense of the word, with 'Miss World', so you will have to tell me who she is. (Mary the Mother of Jesus is my 'Miss Universe', but that's another story). How if Prince Andrew chose you to be his wife?

Sometimes it is not so nice to be chosen, as when the class is asked to do sums in its head, and you all sit there hoping you won't be chosen to give the answer. Or in a theatre, when the conjurer says, 'I want a lady from the audience to come onto the stage and be cut in half,' and you call out, 'Choose Mum!'

2 Since God had promised it

Now God chooses people. He chose Abraham to be the founding father of the Jewish people—we still call them the chosen race. He chose Mary to be the Mother of his Son Jesus. He chooses men and women and boys and girls in each generation to be his saints. But you mustn't think that because God chooses people he has favourites. They are not chosen to be made a fuss of, but chosen for certain

7

work on God's behalf. Certainly with the ones I have mentioned—Abraham, Our Lady Mary, and the saints—it involved them in much suffering and hardship. In a wonderful sort of way he chooses all of us, because he has something special for each of us to do. And this is one way in which belonging to the Church is unlike belonging to anything else. You *choose* to be a Scout or Guide. And you *choose* whether or not to be confirmed ('It must be *your* choice,' I say, 'not anybody choosing for you'). But if you have any awareness at all, you realize that *this* choice of yours has been made in *response*. We are drawn to follow Jesus, we are attracted, we are called. Jesus says, 'You have not chosen me—I have chosen you'.

It is very easy at first to imagine that God was obviously very sensible in choosing you, and what a lot you can do for him. But the other side is also true—it is what he wants to do for you.

3 *If we believe in him*

How does God make his choosing known? How does a woman or girl hear God calling her to some special work, or a man or boy hear the call to be a priest? God doesn't ring them up on the telephone and say, 'Drop everything and do this'. No, God makes them aware of circumstances and needs. He uses other people to suggest and encourage and help to choose. So that gradually the question changes from, 'Why should I do this?' to 'Why shouldn't I?' And I think that is true of any Christian calling, perhaps whether or not to be confirmed. The worry over the decision, the doubts, the hesitations, are all part of the process. And then we say 'Yes, I make my choice, this is what I shall do.'

Only to find Christ before you, choosing you, and our choice a response to him. For Christ says not only, 'Before Abraham was born, I am', but to each of us, 'You have not chosen me, but I have chosen you'.

Sometimes grown-ups say things like, 'Oh, that was before you were thought of'. And that really does cut the ground from beneath your feet—to think that there was a time when you were not the object of someone's love and care. But God never does say that to us. Indeed he says, 'Before you were born I knew you.' And Jesus says, 'Before you were born, I AM.' For we know Jesus to be the eternal Son of the Father, ever to be worshipped and adored.

SIXTH SUNDAY BEFORE CHRISTMAS

In God's house

Hebrews 3.1–6 (TEV)

1 *Who builds a house*

Friday night at the vicarage is banns of marriage night, as some of you have discovered on coming innocently to visit me, and finding yourselves filling in a banns form before we realize who it is. We shall see the couples many times before the actual wedding, but there is little to discuss at this point except the date and time of the coming nuptials. But in extending the conversation a bit I usually ask, 'Have you got anywhere to live yet?' It is rather encouraging that very few couples say 'No' outright. A lot of care and thought has gone into that very need, because it is a very basic need which drives them to seek a house and make their own home.

Seeking a home is one of the basic drives which motivate human beings. One other very obvious one is hunger. The true end of this instinct is the health and survival of the species. We who have never been hungry—you may have been peckish at times, but never hungry—are hardly aware of the strength of this instinct, and what it will make people do under stress. The sexual instinct is a wild and unruly drive, but on it depends the reproduction of the race. But one of the strongest of all is the instinct for territory. We are familiar with the way that

9

animals and birds mark out their territory with scent and sound, and defend it to the death. Human beings share the strength of this feeling, we are indeed the only species which goes to war to increase our territory beyond our immediate needs, even being too close to each other in a lift gives rise to strange reactions. A child will explore the confines of its cot. Old people need something of their own even in a strange place. We want a place to call our own; it is a need to belong which precedes all the other instincts and outlives them all.

2 *What we long for*

If you have ever been homesick (and who hasn't?) you will know how all the little unconsidered things that make up our surroundings are suddenly seen to have supreme value when we are deprived of them. Seaside bungalows are full of people homesick for what they could never list nor describe, but would recognize instantly, like slipping on an old glove. If we can enter into that feeling we can begin to understand a lot of old Testament history. God used this sense of belonging to hold the Jews faithful to him. It was their covenant with God to know and be known by him, but linked always with a particular geographical area. Hence the strength of the drive which stretches through history right from the Exodus to the modern state of Israel. It was part of their discipline that they should rarely enjoy this country, indeed be exiled from it for generations at a time: 'Moses was faithful in God's house as a servant, and he spoke of the things that God would say in the future.' You will recognize instantly the homesickness of Psalm 137: 'By the waters of Babylon we sat down and wept. . . . How shall we sing the Lord's song in a strange land?'

But we do not need the whole stretch of history to recognize the way God works. To each individual Christian he allows a sense of belonging. It is no accident that he gives us a Church or a group of people in which we are especially 'at home'—what a good expression that is!

10

And when we understand the way God deals with us, we discover that all the things we long for in this life are really looking forward to beyond this life altogether, which is why we are never fully satisfied now. It is as if God said, 'You really belong to me, but because you forget this I give you reminders. I give you this great sense of belonging as a sort of sample. But it will never completely satisfy you—only I can do that.'

There is a further lesson, that this treasure of knowing God, of belonging to him, of being at home with him, and being filled with an inexpressible longing for the fulfilment which can come only with him—this is not just for us, but is God's will for all men. Our intimacy with God is not a cosy contracting out of life, but is meant to be a dynamic relationship. We are drawn to be at home with God so that we can share him with others.

3 God has built all things

> Moses was faithful in God's house as a servant . . . but Christ is faithful as the Son in charge of God's house. We are his house if we keep up our courage and our confidence in what we hope for.

Imagine that you are a house. You know that there are things wrong with you: dry rot here, a blocked drain there. You are pleased when the builders are called in, God and Son. And you are pleased when the dry rot is cured and the drains are cleared. But you discover that the builders do not leave. They are opening sealed doors and jammed windows, they are building extensions and throwing out new wings. You thought you would be put in order and then left alone. But God has no intention of leaving you comfortable. He is building a palace. He intends to come and live in you himself.

11

FIFTH SUNDAY BEFORE CHRISTMAS

Something to say to you Gentiles

Romans 11.13–24 (NEB)

1 *The whole lump*

Among the better programmes brought into our homes by television are those which help us to understand the world in which we live, and which help us to understand ourselves more clearly. I am thinking at the moment of the 'World About Us' kind of programme, which explores the wonders of nature and sometimes explores the life of some primitive tribe of Stone Age man which has survived into the twentieth century, hidden and unchanged. What you discover about man is that he has always been incurably religious—by which I mean that he seems always to have been conscious of a reality greater than himself, always aware that he lived on the borderland between the known and the vastly greater unknown.

There are several ways in which we get hints of this. One is that wherever man has been able to live a settled domestic life, the way in which he has buried his dead has shown some glimmer of awareness that death is not extinction. But we see the religious instinct at work not only in the face of death, but at all the great turning points of life: birth, maturity, marriage; what are known in the anthropologist trade as 'rites of passage'. Faced with the deep mysteries of birth, fertility and death, man has always known that they provide a profound statement about his own existence, what it means to be human. He is moved to *wonder*, and wonder is a religious instinct. So he surrounds these rites of passage with ceremony. And who is to tell when religion and superstition overlap? For faced with mystery man acts either in a religious way (that is, he responds with awe and worship), or he reacts in a superstitious way (that is, he tries to appease the powers and control events, or at the least avert disaster).

The rites of passage are communal affairs, for they

12

involve the survival of the tribe. So a birth is welcomed by the whole clan; the fertility of the maturing young is ensured by the correct tribal ceremonies; marriage and death are tribal occasions.

2 *Men of my own race*

Now although I have been describing the 'world about us' as a survival of the past, it is clear to us all that I have been holding up a mirror to ourselves. For although we no longer kill our food with stone axes we are still human, and being human we still face the same mysteries of life and death. We are still *religious* creatures. Nor does it take long for us to slip from religion into superstition (touch wood). The demand for babies to be baptized is motivated at its lowest level by the need for some family occasion, and recognition of its newest member. We still 'come of age,' although a discreet party in the Union Hotel is no match for what used to go on in the bushes. We hang horseshoes round the necks of brides. There is a formality about bereavement and death which is only proper.

As you travel around the world you discover that the great family of man has the same family likeness wherever he lives. In a Hindu society the rites of passage have a Hindu flavour; in an Islamic country an Islamic expression; in a Christian society a Christian expression. But underlying them all there is something in common, because we share a common humanity and have in common one creator. These expressions are now called 'folk religion', but the traditionally better title is 'natural religion'.

3 *Not superior to the branches*

There are at least two mistakes we could make about all this as the Christian community in this town. One would be to be cynical about people's religious urges and make jokes about 'four-wheel Christians', who come to church only in a pram, a wedding car, or a hearse. If we have nothing to say to people at the deep moments of their lives we are not being Christlike. Another mistake would be to become an exclusive clique, to raise the drawbridge and say, 'you can cross only if you have the right password'. For we live, as always with Christian things, with a paradox—the paradox of the *demands* of the Gospel, and the *welcome* of the Gospel. Had we not known the welcome for ourselves we would not be here; but, although our heavenly Father is easily *pleased*, he will never be *satisfied* until we love him completely for his own sake.

The society in which we live in the 1980s in this country is still residually Christian in its attitudes and beliefs, but far from being Christian in the sense that *we* understand it, in a personal relationship with God through Jesus, living in the stream of the Holy Spirit. Yet it is exactly at the turning points of life and death that people come to the Church for the rites of passage. I invite you to consider how far they really want *Christian* rites, and how far they are acting at the level of natural religion. People come to me because I am the local priest. How far am I regarded as a Christian priest, and how far just as a cultic figure to perform the correct cultic acts?

It has always been simple for the Church to be the Church in a completely hostile environment. It has always been easy (though dangerous) for the Church to be the Church in a completely Christian society. We have the more difficult task of living in an indifferent society, but a society which still demands Christian rites.

As Christians we share natural religion, but live and worship within the context of revealed religion. We know why man is naturally religious. It is because God made us that way. However much human sin, the fall of man, has obscured the truth, it has never completely obliterated man's awareness of life greater than himself. As Christians we know not only that God has made us for himself, but that in his Son, Jesus Christ, he has shared our humanity, that we may share his divinity. Christianity is not one religion among many, it is the explanation and

14

fulfilment of all religion: in Christ the author himself walks onto the stage. This is why in the best meaning of the word we call the Church 'catholic'—it comprehends all religion, explains it, fulfils it, redeems it.

Observe the kindness and the severity of God . . . it is in God's power to graft them in again.

ADVENT SUNDAY

About dates and times

1 Thessalonians 5.1–11 (NEB)

1 *Doom on the doorstep*

The little woman stands on the doorstep. There is in her eye a glint of determination which alerts your mental alarm system.

. . . all at once calamity is upon them . . . and there will be no escape.

'You would agree, would you not,' she asks, 'that there is distress among the nations? See: it is all predicted in the Bible.'

Your mental alarm system is now clanging away. You are faced, you realise with sinking heart, with a little woman who is a Jehovah's Witness.

'I'm not sure,' you mumble, 'that I want anything to do with hell and judgement—I go to St Mary's.'

O wise and gentle Christian, if you can then charitably but firmly shut the door. If not, you are in for a long haul. For your open heart makes you particularly vulnerable to an expert and persistent form of salesmanship.

And there is an elementary equation which applies to all argument and persuasion, that far more deadly than

15

the lie (the deliberate untruth), far more deadly is the half-truth, for the half which is true already has a foothold in your mind.

2 *The wrath of God*

Yes, there does run through the Bible the theme of judgement, of the righteousness of God being vindicated. It is a theme particularly of the season of Advent, which we enter today. There *is* a wrath of God against all unrighteousness and sin. It is a high and terrible doctrine inescapable from his utter holiness.

This is the half of the truth demonstrated by our little woman on the doorstep, who claims to be a witness of Jehovah, who is the God of the Old Testament. She descends in that tradition which covered the walls of medieval churches with pictures of the last judgement, of hell and of torture.

'Yes,' you say to her, 'you are the witness of Jehovah, of the Old Testament, but you see only half. I am a witness of Jesus Christ, of the New Testament. Here is a deeper mystery. For in Jesus we see God himself suffering the penalty of sin and paying its price. The righteousness of God is vindicated, not one element of his wrath against unrighteousness and sin is removed. But here is the greater half of the truth, that though the sin will repel God to the end of time, his love for the sinner exceeds your prophecies of doom, and makes nonsense of your arithmetic of the elect.'

3 *God's true purpose*

> God has not destined us to the terrors of judgement but to the full attainment of salvation through our Lord Jesus Christ.

In the true tradition of doom painting our dear Lord is depicted not as an irritated magistrate, but as standing simply there, showing the wounds of his Passion, as if saying, 'All this I have done for you'.

16

'Dear lady,' you say, as you gently close the door, 'I take very seriously indeed the possibility of losing God for ever, and I am grateful for your warning, but my only hope is not of being frightened into Kingdom Hall, but of being loved into the kingdom of heaven.'

ADVENT 2

Who your teachers were

    2 Timothy 3.14–4.5 (TEV)

1 *The truths that you were taught*

'Jesus came to Nazareth, where he had been brought up, and went to synagogue on the Sabbath day as he regularly did.' Well, some of us have been to that synagogue in Nazareth ourselves, and it's a rather small and scruffy one now, but the scenery pales into insignificance against the character of the actor who walked onto the stage that day: 'this text is being fulfilled even as you listen'.

It is a scene which was to be reproduced time and time again, only a few years later, as the Christian Gospel spread throughout the Roman Empire in the first century AD. For scattered through the cities of the Roman Empire there were many Jews, who found their national and religious focus (seeing no distinction between the two) in their local synagogue. It was natural for those apostles bringing the news of Christ to go first to these synagogues, to proclaim that Jesus of Nazareth was the fulfilment of all they read, and prayed, and hoped for. Sometimes the Synagogue believed, and became the seed of the local Christian Church; sometimes it remained in opposition; but the message of the apostles was the same as that of Christ himself. 'This text is fulfilled'—in Jesus. In his words and works, in his death and rising again, the things spoken about in the Old Testament—kingdom, messiah, peace, mercy, righteousness, exodus, temple, glory, had

17

now happened, and happened in a way that makes the previous occurrence of them only a pale foretaste.

2 *You have known the holy Scriptures*

Let us underline this by something familiar to us all: Handel's *Messiah*, which moves us to adoration and the joyful kind of tears (well, it moves *me*, soft old thing that I am). Handel's *Messiah* consists largely of passages from the *Old* Testament—'Comfort ye, comfort ye my people', 'I know that my redeemer liveth', to mention just two. But the content, the meaning of those passages, is transformed because we come to them knowing the living Christ, just as the apostles went to the scattered synagogues knowing the living Christ, just as to that synagogue in Nazareth went the living Christ himself.

The fulfilment of the Old Testament is made valid by Christ, not the other way round. What I mean is, we don't believe in Jesus because of what we read in the Old Testament, but knowing Jesus we see unfolding in the Old Testament the loving purposes of God.

This is why as Christians it is right for us to include in our worship parts of the Old Testament, and in these days when the offices of Mattins and Evensong no longer form the staple diet of Christians we welcome into our eucharistic worship the Old Testament lesson. Nor must we lose sight of the Psalms, or my claim will cease to be true, that Anglicans can sing Anglican chants by some special grace absorbed from the British climate.

3 *Salvation through faith in Christ Jesus*

So Christ is the fulfilment not just of biblical texts, not just of the aspirations of the Jews, but of all the longings and searchings of men's hearts since time began. And like all eternal truths, the fulfilment of the Old Testament by Christ is part of the experience of each one of us. I am thinking now of those adults who come each year to the point of confirmation, whom it is such a privilege to help by removing barriers to understanding, and whom we all

18

help insofar as we are a loving and nurturing community. For many of them it has been a long search, but on all dawns the realization that somehow, in Jesus, there is the answer to questions, the fulfilment of hope, and the end of longing. The hints and suggestions and glimpses of truth begin to focus on Christ.

For if Christ *is* God sharing our own life, then he is the fulfilment of every search for truth ever made by man. We don't have to believe that every religion except our own is totally misled, but that all truth is of God; and where truth is seen and followed it leads to Christ (in the next world if not in this) and through Christ to our heavenly Father, since on Christ's own authority, no one comes to the Father except through him. Christians hold this truth in trust for the world.

Into that rather small and scruffy synagogue in Nazareth came Jesus on the Sabbath day, as he regularly did, and he was handed their chief treasure—for the scroll of the Scriptures to this day occupies the place of honour in the assembly—and Jesus took their treasure with reverence and love, and transformed it. 'This text is being fulfilled today even as you listen,' for it speaks of me.

So Jesus comes into our small and rather scruffy lives, and with great reverence and love accepts the secret longing of our heart, and says 'The secret longing of your heart speaks of me. Did you not know?'

ADVENT 3

Stewards of the mysteries of God

1 Corinthians 4.1–5 (RSV)

1 *How one should regard us*

Saint Francis is supposed to have said that should he meet together an angel and a priest (this possibility surprises you, but Francis is a saint)—should this improbability

19

occur, then he would salute first the priest, for he represents Christ himself.

Before we go any further we shall do what we always do when we want to get things straight: we shall go to our Lord himself; because the further we get from him in any discussion or argument, the further are we getting from the point. And it seems that the way we regard the ministers of the Gospel depends very much upon the way we regard the Gospel itself, and the way we regard our priests depends very much on our attitude to the great high priest, Jesus himself.

If of course you think the whole of the Christian faith a sham, then the clergy become either the victims of this deception or its perpetrators, and are in either case most despicable.

If you think that the Christian faith is simply obedience to a moral code, being as good as your neighbour, and kind to your mother-in-law and not kicking the cat downstairs, then the clergy become the prim upholders of an outdated morality, and are either prudes because they observe it, or hypocrites because they don't.

If you think our Lord came to the human race merely as a great teacher and example, then the clergy become the ethical buttresses of the nation, and are thought on the whole to be a good thing by those who want society to stay as it is. These are the people who like religious education in schools because they imagine it keeps their daughters out of trouble and their sons' hair short.

2 *Servants of Christ*

But if you have any inkling in your bones that Jesus is not a dead hero but a living Lord, that in him God enters his own creation—not to tell nice stories nor set a good example, but to save men and women from the hell of separation from God, that his body the Church continues this saving work as once his human body achieved it, that we are called into this body by a definite act of his love, that the Church is a vast family spanning earth and

20

paradise and heaven, that there will come a time when God will have used the world to his purpose, and all nations and cultures and even the human race will be extinct, but we shall be alive within this family, and will remember the world as an old tale: then we begin haltingly and with awe to acknowledge the vision of Christ to be true, which sees him high and lifted up, wonderful, counsellor, mighty God, the prince of peace, king of kings and lord of lords, our great high priest.

3 *Windows into heaven*

In ordaining priests we are not playing archaic games. We are furthering the saving work of Christ himself, who expresses his priesthood through the whole body of the Church, and the Church expresses its priesthood through those whom she sets aside and ordains.

Think ahead now to when you will kneel at this altar rail, and in your mind's eye picture the altar rail not ending at the north or south walls, but continuing round to encircle all the altars of the Church throughout the world, so that as you kneel there you are kneeling side by side with the fellow members of God's family all over the world. To each local community within the great family our Lord himself comes in all his living power when the priest speaks the words of Jesus 'this is my Body, this is my Blood'.

This is the family of the Church at worship as we see it, from our point of view. But Christ is not divided, there is not one Christ for each altar of holy Church. Open the eyes of your soul now, and try to see that as you kneel at the altar rail you have your elbows on the very window sills of heaven itself. There are not hundreds and hundreds of eucharists going on, there is only one—the eternal offering of himself being made by our Lord before the throne of heaven, and it is in this that we all join when we obey his command to 'do this'. We are all looking the same way, all joining in the same thing, with angels and archangels and all the company of heaven.

21

The priests God gives us, he gives so that they may open the windows of heaven to us. That is why it is such a frightening privilege to be a priest, because through no desert of one's own one pleads the sacrifice of Christ, which is the only thing in this mad bad world of ours which has done any real good. This is why the treasure of the priesthood is honoured, though it is a treasure carried in very grubby earthen vessels.

Saint Francis is supposed to have said that should he meet together an angel and a priest, he would salute first the priest, for in him he sees Christ himself.

We priests may perhaps keep company with angels, but we shall not be met by many saints. Many of those among whom we go have their eyes fixed firmly on this world, and are unaware of the glorious reality which lies just out of sight. When we speak of life we hear angels, they hear only us. When we speak of the Church we see visions, but they see only us. We must so conduct ourselves that these erring, precious, children of God never say to us in vain, 'Sir, we would see Jesus'.

ADVENT 4

Boast of what the Lord has done

    1 Corinthians 1.26–end (TEV)

1 Remember what you were

There was a time when I shared digs with a medical student and his skeleton. And every day, before the landlady's little boy came in, we took great care to hide the skeleton lest the child have nightmares. It was only quite by chance that we found out that he knew about it all the time, and was the hero of his school for having a skeleton in the cupboard at home.

Of course, every good home has a skeleton in the cupboard, and a more robust generation didn't mind admitting it. Do you remember all those 'begats': 'Abraham begat Isaac, and Isaac begat Jacob. . . ' through many generations until you got to 'and Matthan begat Jacob, and Jacob begat Joseph the husband of Mary, of whom was born Jesus, who is called Christ'?

We are left to conclude that Mary and Joseph were of the same kin, for the genealogy is his, not hers, but no one quarrels with that conclusion. Let us think what it implies. It implies that on his mother's side Jesus was descended from a pretty rough line, with its share of blackguards and its share of skeletons in the family cupboard. What sinners figure in the birth-roll of the Son of God: Jacob, who deceived his father and cheated his brother; Judah and Tamar, whose union was incestuous; Rahab the harlot, who like Ruth later was not even of the chosen race; David himself, adulterer and murderer; Solomon and Rehoboam—these were among the fathers of humanity, the individuals from whom the Son of God chose to receive his manhood. And coming out of them, and linking him to them, Mary of Nazareth.

2 *To shame the wise*

The emergence of Mary full of grace, out of humanity in general and from the seed of Abraham and house of David in particular, recalls the picture of the refiner's pot—the crucible over which the refiner of silver sits, until the dross is burnt away, the pure metal rises to the surface, and he sees his likeness mirrored in it.

As to how God brought her, unique, apt for his purpose as she was, how he brought her out of our sinful race, some may think one thing, some another; others again may feel that any theorizing about a mystery so secret and holy savours of rushing in where angels fear to tread. But to the fact of Mary, and God's loving purpose in preparing her, all Christians bow down.

Mary's Son said later that no one could enter the kingdom of heaven, save by coming as a little child. His blessed Mother, as the gospels show her, perfectly displays that childlike character. She has the absolute forthright simplicity and the unquestioning trust of a young child. She has this unqualified delight in knowing that the Lord her God is pleased with her.

Because the gospels we have do not share our modern obsession with 'biography', with knowing the intimate secrets of the great, it was not long before what are known as the Apocryphal Gospels began to appear. These were motivated no doubt by piety; but piety is the mother of invention, and few of these apocryphal gospels ring true. One of them, however, which by tradition comes from St James, has some things in it which are not like that. One is that when her parents brought Mary to the temple at the age of three 'she danced with her feet, and all Israel loved her'. Even if we cannot vouch for its authenticity it suggests the sort of child she surely must have been, brimming with energy and *joie de vivre*.

That is the Mary I like to picture, not the wan prissy figure of repository art, but someone manifestly more alive than anyone else.

3 *We become God's holy people*

We are looking forward now to Christmas. The Lord who comes to me in my Communion and to you in yours, and the Lord who came to Mary on Lady Day, are one Lord and the same. He came to Mary that his incarnation might begin; he comes to us that his incarnation may be extended. The difference between her and us is in response: she from the first so utterly at his disposal; we so ill-prepared.

Yet whatever skeleton we may have in our own cupboard he goes on coming to us:

> By him we are put right with God; we become God's holy people and are set free.

We boast of what the Lord has done. 'She danced with her feet, and all Israel loved her.' And so do we.

24

SUNDAY AFTER CHRISTMAS DAY

No longer a slave but a son

Galatians 4.1–7 (NEB)

1 *God incarnate*

'Incarnate' is a technical word, and it is worth unravelling what it really means. At its heart, as with so many words we use, it is a bit of Latin—'carnis', 'flesh'. The Word was made flesh.

So it's Jonathan Miller and 'The Body in Question'—all that slippery, pulsating system which supports our life. It includes all this, but it is more than this. It is everything we mean by 'human nature'—the life of the mind too, and the life of the spirit.

After all, when you say you know old Joe, it isn't just his gastric juices you are talking about, but the whole 'Joe-ness' of him: his freckles, his short-sightedness, the way he gets on with his wife, his fears of becoming redundant, his ambitions and his failures, why he's here at all.

So when we talk about God becoming incarnate it is not something remote we are talking about. It is something far more basic, far more immediate, far closer home.

2 *And so it was with us*

If God did take the raw material of human nature to himself it says some impressive things about human nature.

First, it knocks on the head any idea that you can separate sacred things from unsacred, or secular, things. If God can do this to his creation, then everything is sacred. I can't divide my life up and say, 'This bit belongs to God, and this bit belongs to me.' Or 'What I do in church is one thing, and how I spend the day with my family another thing altogether.' There is, we discover, a wholeness about things, a wholeness demonstrated at

Bethlehem, and the whole belongs to God. It is not a different world from ours that God entered at Bethlehem, it is the same one.

Secondly, the way we organize our lives together must be of concern to God. This raises the whole question of the Church and politics. Christians will disagree, like everyone else, about the way to organize society (and what is 'politics' but the art of living together?), but they are all concerned about the purposes and aims of society—because at Bethlehem God entered not only a stable, but a political situation. The incarnate life was lived out in an occupied country, and ended with a particularly horrid form of public execution. It is not a different world from ours that God entered at Bethlehem, it is the same one.

With my third I tread on sensitive ground, because all this has implications for the bit of human nature we know best—I mean our own. Because of what God did at Bethlehem our humanity is seen to be precious to him. Our bodies—these strange lusting, demanding, things, which are our frontiers with other people—these are precious, they are holy. It does matter what we do with our humanity, and the way we use or abuse our minds and bodies. We may not agree on abortion or smoking or crash helmets or mental trash, but we can agree that we are answerable for the way we use our bodies, and the way we use other people.

But this is easy polemic. Let us rather see the loving purpose of God shining even in our darkest places.

Take any five hundred people. By the law of averages, fifty-four would have spent some time in mental care, thirty men or women would have been completely homosexual, two hundred and three affected in some way by marriage difficulty, the temperament of sixty-two would have been so difficult that it would have caused distress to ourselves or others, and of those with one hang-up or another I should estimate that there were five hundred!

It is the deepest conviction of Christian experience that

26

God-incarnate-at-Bethlehem has something profound not only to *say* about our condition, but something profound to *do* about it.

3 *By God's own act an heir*

Look, instead of always thinking of God coming to us, can we try to imagine what it looks like from his point of view? So that we see Jesus bringing our human nature to our heavenly Father. To come to the Father is the only reason for our existence. There is no other.

Because of what happened at Bethlehem (for it was our same world he took to himself) we know that we can have no salvation apart from our human nature. It has got to be with it and through it. And 'salvation' means 'wholeness', to which is related 'health'.

When Jesus is accepted as our constant companion, he is always the other dimension in our home, in our marriage, in our sexual nature, in our pains and despairs, and in our joys and delights. It is not by contracting out of life that we discover God, but in the rough and tumble of it. And where we discover Jesus we have a grip on sanity and wholesomeness, the beginning of wholeness, the beginning of health, the beginning of salvation. Because ours is the human nature he has taken to himself at Bethlehem. It is not a different world he entered, but the same one.

> *To prove that you are sons, God has sent into our hearts the Spirit of his Son, crying 'Abba! Father!' You are therefore no longer a slave but a son, and if a son, then also by God's own act an heir.*

SECOND SUNDAY AFTER CHRISTMAS

Holy and unholy fear

Romans 8.11–17 (RSV)

1 *To fall back into fear*

The other Sunday evening the Junior Youth Club was visited by two policemen and a big dog. This, I hasten to add, was by invitation. Part of the handler's *spiel* was to explain how dogs can scent our fear. By this time, of course, I was on top of the cupboard, with two rows of innocent children between me and this monster. Perfect love, says St Paul, casts out fear, but I was glad when it was the dog which went.

Ordinary fear is one of the basic human emotions. It has physical symptoms: we go clammy; the skin of our skull contracts so that our hair stands on end; glands inject into the bloodstream chemicals which speed up our responses and thereby make it easier to climb onto cupboards; we even smell different. True bravery is when men act in spite of their fears. As we see quite clearly in war, the truly brave man is not so much the reckless idiot, as the sensitive and imaginative man who yet looks fear in the eye. 'Good dog!' I say.

2 *If the Spirit dwells in you*

A week after this brush with the law the Bishop was here in church at the Confirmation, and you will remember how on such an occasion he recites that very ancient prayer for the gifts of the Spirit: wisdom, understanding, counsel, inward strength, knowledge, true godliness; 'and let their delight be in the fear of the Lord'. What does that mean? At the thought of God should we go clammy and our hair stand on end? but in a holy sort of way? are we meant to be afraid of God?

You know, there are people in whose religion this kind

28

of fear has a large place. I don't mean now primitive man, jumping at the sound of the wind, placating the god of this and the god of that, whose local counterpart is the superstitious man 'touching wood'. There are Christians who practise their religion out of a fear of the consequences of doing otherwise; there are those whose only virtue comes from fear of doing wrong. This fear of hell, servile fear, sometimes has a place in waking men to the consequences of their sins, so it is not to be despised. But it remains human fear, and not holy fear. A stage higher is filial fear, the fear of offending a Father's love. Filial fear will not make us frightened, just more careful.

It is best to think of Holy Fear as the awe we should feel before God. It is reverence before his majesty and wonder:

> you did not receive the spirit of slavery to fall back into fear, but you have received the spirit of sonship. When we cry, 'Abba! Father!' it is the Spirit himself bearing witness with our spirit that we are children of God.

3 *The spirit of sonship*

Now in a person in whom the gift of holy fear is growing we should be able to discern these things.

First, he or she is able to speak about God in a way which is neither servile nor presumptuous. I mean this: the gulf between God who creates and ourselves who are created is the biggest gulf there can be. It is, in fact, a gulf which God himself has bridged, but he remains unimaginably more GOD than we dare allow ourselves to think. We have been given the freedom of children, but we are royal children in the palace of our King, and the Christian carries this awareness as a sense of privilege.

Secondly, this reverence for God rubs off on to the things of God. For instance, a church, because it is one place where we undoubtedly receive the gifts of God, is treated with reverence, as are the sacraments. The one thing we don't joke about is Holy Communion. This is reflected in our outward acts of reverence. We are careful about the way we walk and kneel and sit in church. An outward sloppiness or casualness usually reveals an inward sloppiness and casualness, and the converse can be true. I know these things can become habits, like the overwhelming desire to genuflect to the screen in a cinema, but there are good habits as well as bad ones. We take our religion very seriously, but don't take ourselves too seriously.

Thirdly, in a person in whom this gift of holy fear is growing, there will be developing a true courtesy and reverence for other people. They too are seen in this same light of everything being given by God. 'Next time,' said William Temple, 'you think a person not worth bothering about, remember that Christ thought him worth dying for!' Our reverence for all things is part of our reverence for him who makes them, and this is immeasurably intensified when we come to persons: this is the flesh which in Christ was raised to the Godhead, and is after this for ever glorified.

> *we are heirs of God and fellow heirs with Christ,*
> *provided we suffer with him in order that we may also*
> *be glorified with him.*

There is no contradiction between love and holy fear. The depth of our reverence will reveal the depth of our love, and the habits of outward reverence will help inward love to grow.

> *Then I heard all the living things in creation crying 'to*
> *the One who is sitting on the throne and to the Lamb,*
> *be all praise, honour, glory and power, for ever and*
> *ever,' and the elders prostrated themselves to worship.*

30

EPIPHANY 1

In every nation

Acts 10.34–38a (NEB)

1 *His word to the Israelites*

The Jordan valley is part of one of those natural faults on
the earth's surface. The river Jordan flows down it,
through the Sea of Galilee and beyond, finally losing itself
in the Dead Sea, the lowest point on the earth's surface,
1300 feet below sea level. There used to be a hotel there
which advertised itself as 'The Lowest Hotel on Earth'.

In the hills around the western shores of the Dead Sea
are the caves where what are known as 'the Dead Sea
Scrolls' were found in 1947. What happened in 1947 was
that a shepherd boy, looking for a lost goat, had thrown
stones into a cave, trying to flush it out. In one cave he
was rewarded by a 'clunk-click' sound, not as the goat
fastened its seat-belt, but as the stone hit and broke a jar.
In the stone jars he then discovered many ancient scrolls.
The skins, the parchment, on which the Prophecies of
Isaiah were written, were of no interest to him, and he
sold them to a cobbler. By an amazing sequence of events
their true worth was discovered. They were the scriptures
of a religious community living on the shores of the Dead
Sea before and during the time of Jesus. The 'Essenes',
as they were known, had withdrawn from the compromising life under Roman occupation, and were living lives of
strict discipline in that forbidding country at Qumran.

As the crow flies (a demented crow to fly anywhere in
that climate!) it is less than eight miles from Qumran to
Bethabara, one of the fords across the Jordan, still
pointed out today as the place where John baptized Jesus.
To this close geographical nearness we add a spiritual
nearness, for the Essenes also issued a call to repentance, and for their departure into the wilderness they
appealed to the very passage of Isaiah on which John the
Baptist based his ministry: 'A voice cries, prepare in the

wilderness a way for the Lord, make a straight highway for our God across the desert.' We needn't be surprised therefore at the suggestion of some kind of link between John and the Essenes, if only that they shared the same spiritual climate, and this without in any way detracting from the uniqueness of his call as the forerunner of Jesus.

2 *The man who is godfearing*

I paint in this background purposely. We are provided each Sunday with a neat little capsule of gospel narrative, and the temptation is to think of this event, or that saying, in isolation—tempted today, perhaps, to think of John the Baptist as starting from scratch. Whereas, far from starting from scratch, there was a consciousness among the people everywhere, but most obviously with a community like the Essenes; there was a consciousness, and a conscience, to which he could appeal, and which would recognize his baptism as a cleansing of the people of God for the fulfilment of God's purpose. Within the providence of God, this meeting of Jesus and John in the waters of the River Jordan was the culminating point to which generations of prophecy and holiness had led.

Now there is a pattern in the affairs of God, a shape in the way God goes about things, which this episode illustrates, and which is really the point I want to make. John the Baptist was a man seized by God; but the seizing took place within the context and expectations of a worshipping community. Before he was born, his father Zacharias had had a vision of his son's vocation, but he received this vision while he was about his normal duties in the temple—it was his turn on duty, he was the 'Canon in Residence'.

And so it always is. If a man comes up to you, and you know his only experience of the Church is family weddings and funerals, you have some natural doubts if he says, 'I think God wants me to be Archbishop of Canterbury'. No, in trying to recognize a genuine call or vocation, the first thing you look for is stability in the

32

ordinary humdrum things of the Christian life—saying your prayers, receiving the sacraments, showing the fruits of the Spirit.

If we really want to know what God wants us to do, we are more likely to become aware of it, not by sitting around waiting for flashes of inspiration, but simply by getting on with saying our prayers and worshipping with the Christian community. As St John says, we get to know God by doing his will. We may have a lot of walking to do before we can begin to run, but walking does at least maintain progress.

I don't know that Christian obedience is a very fashionable idea nowadays, but the essence of it is not a great crisis of conscience if the Vicar asks you to do something. Far more it is simply getting on with the next thing which our life in the Christian community puts before us.

3 God has no favourites

The other point worth noting is that whereas we re-member the shepherd boy who threw the stone which broke the jar which gave up its secret, the men who made the jar and hid it and its precious contents—they are known only to God. Yet it was their faith and their faithfulness which set the stage for John the Baptist, who prepared the way for Christ. Without the supporting cast the play could not go on. Without the chorus the soloists could not perform. Each of us is unique, but we are not isolated. If we could bring back that crow for a moment and take a bird's eye view of Christian history we should see the value to God of the faithful community. It is the faithful community, doing ordinary things faithfully, which enables God to do great things.

There were centuries of preparation before God could say, 'This is my Son, my Beloved, on whom my favour rests,' or St Peter could say, 'You know about Jesus of Nazareth, how God anointed him with the Holy Spirit and with power'. There were generations of countless, unknown, ordinary people, though each is known by God. Don't worry about being ordinary. God must like ordinary people—he made so many of them!

EPIPHANY 2

Travelling to Damascus

Acts 26.1,9–20 (NEB)

1 *As I was on my way*

We can think of many journeys in the Scriptures, because the Christian understanding of life sees it as a journey, a pilgrimage, a progress; not going round and round again as the reincarnationists believe, but getting from here to there. Indeed the nickname for the early Christians was 'followers of the way,' from one of the great I AM sayings of Jesus, you remember (well I do, because it is one of the set readings for funerals):

> *Jesus said to his disciples, 'Set your troubled hearts at rest. Believe in God; believe also in me. In my Father's house are many rooms; if it were not so I would have told you. And after I have gone and prepared a place for you I will come again and take you to myself, so that where I am you may be also. And where I am going you know, and the way you know.' Thomas said, 'Lord we do not know where you are going; how can we know the way?' Jesus said to him, 'I AM the way, the truth and the life. No one comes to the Father but by me.' (John 14.1–6, TEV)*

In our journey through life we have many companions and helpers on the way, and I invite you to reflect on some of them today—people who have made Jesus known to you; people you can look back to, and with the long sight of memory realize how they have helped you on

34

the way, whether or not they were conscious of it. And if I tell you about one of mine it is one way I can show my gratitude, and it may help you to be grateful for your helpers too.

2 *I send you to open their eyes*

Some years ago I was in St Albans Cathedral for the enthronement of Robert Runcie as Bishop of St Albans, and it is one of the strange historical quirks of the Church of England that bishops in the southern province are always put in their place by the Archdeacon of Canterbury—sent by the boss I suppose to make sure it is done properly. And I suddenly recognized in the then Archdeacon of Canterbury a priest I had last known when he was a young curate in my home parish where I had been a choirboy. It had been one of his tasks, poor man, to run a Bible Class on Sunday afternoons. The point of my story is this: he was the first person I became conscious of who spoke of Jesus not as a figure in the past, but as a living friend in his own life. He was no tub-thumper, and he never laboured the point. It was simply the way he used the words 'Our Lord' that got through to a callow youth. I hadn't spoken to him then, had not seen him for all those years, and had no chance to speak to him when I saw him again. He wouldn't even know who I am, and only when he gets to heaven will he ever be aware of being a helper on my way.

Now that is an encouraging tale for choirboys, for curates, and not least for archdeacons, about whose salvation there is constant doubt!

3 *I appoint you my servant and witness*

'Prove the Resurrection!' people say. And our proof is the countless number of perfectly ordinary people to whom Jesus is not a dead hero, but a living Lord, and who demonstrate that knowledge not necessarily in saying a lot about it, but simply by the sort of people they are. They are the true Easter people.

Well, that is my recollection, refreshed after many years. You have your own, when you first became aware of someone in touch with God, knowing that until you sorted the whole thing out you would never know the meaning of life. And like St Paul on the Damascus Road you were aware of God taking the initiative—oh, all that talk about 'man seeking God,' when the whole Christian experience is of being sought *by* God, and being attracted by him! There are many of you—there is no need to go seeking in the past for examples—who so obviously keep company with Jesus, that without your knowing it Christ speaks through you to others.

In a few moments we shall be singing the Creed, and telling everybody that 'we believe in one holy catholic and apostolic Church'. Let us 'unwrap', as they say, the word 'apostolic': the Church built on the foundation of the apostles and prophets, Jesus Christ being the chief corner-stone—yes, we know that; the Church handing on authority by the vast network of the apostolic succession, spanning time and eternity—yes, we know that too. But consider for a moment the original qualification for an apostle within the life of the early Church. It was not only that he should have kept company with Jesus, but that he should have been a witness of the Resurrection, a witness of Jesus alive. St Paul, an apostle 'as one born out of due time' was not disobedient to the heavenly vision.

Will people say of us in forty, fifty, years' time, 'I first learned from him, from her, to know Jesus as a living friend—not so much from what they said, you know, but from the kind of people they were'?

And so, King Agrippa, I did not disobey the heavenly vision. I . . . sounded the call to repent and turn to God, and to prove their repentance by deeds.

36

EPIPHANY 3

Christian unity

> *1 John 1.1–7 (TEV)*

1 *Walking on the past*

In 1865 a new road in Penzance was constructed from Alverton to the sea. Its name commemorates the Princess of Wales who opened it: Alexandra Road.

And wherever we walk, we walk on history: Albert Dock, Battery Road, Coinage Hall Street, Quarry Gardens, the Ropewalk; the past is always with us, helping to shape the pattern of our town and the pattern of our lives. The more ancient past of Cornwall thrusts itself into the present with rocky outcrop and sacred spring still springing. If you look at old maps you see how ancient fields and boundaries still live on in present names.

Our present is shaped by the past, whether or not we are aware of it. Even the sort of people we are has its root in our very experience of birth.

And this is true also of our politics and religion. Although our individual relationship with God is unique, we do not come to him as isolated individuals, but within a Christian community which has history and continuity with the past. With the pure milk of the Word we also drink in a set of assumptions and unexamined habits.

This is why new, enquiring, Christians are so refreshing: 'Why do you do that?' they ask, of something we do in church which to us has become automatic. 'Oh,' I say, 'some curate years ago made me do it!' But there are many other things we do, and we do them in certain ways, whose origins are lost in the past. Any real meeting with fellow Christians, any genuine openness, will force us to examine many of our assumptions and attitudes.

For there are two ways in which we can be slaves to history. The first is by being ignorant of it, for those ignorant of history are condemned to re-live its mistakes.

You can begin to understand the town you live in only when you know something of its past; you can begin to understand yourself only when you unravel the assumptions you inherit.

The other way we can be slaves to history is by closing our minds to change and going on fighting old battles. Circumstances alter. The wandering cattle-tracks of Cornwall and the narrow streets of its towns were once sufficient, but they inhibit the pace and flow of modern life.

2 *A new thing*

You will recall how when the Pope's visit to this country was proposed the battlelines of the past began to reassert themselves, as people lined themselves up on the boundaries of old disputes, in the end to be out-flanked by God, by the God of creation, who said 'Behold I do a new thing!' Pope and Archbishop kissed the Gospels at Canterbury, and nothing can be the same again.

Several years before that, Westminster Abbey celebrated its nine hundred years of history, and as part of the celebrations the Roman Catholic monks of Downside sang Vespers in the Abbey. And the newspapers began to fill with letters of protest from those who do protest about such things, and the letters said things like 'If religion isn't about truth it isn't about anything'. But this correspondence was closed by a quiet letter from the then Bishop of Manchester, who said, 'The Christian Faith is not about truth, it is about him who said "I am the Truth".'

In the Church we are not members of a static institution, but living members of an organism, growing, developing—becoming, please God, ever more mature in Christ.

The path to unity has echoed to the noise of collapsing schemes of unification. We shall probably look back in years to come and draw all the lessons from this that we need to learn. But one thing that does come through loud and clear already is that unity cannot mean uniformity, all being alike, and doing things in the same way. And once we accept that divisions are within the body and not from it, we see other creative tensions right through Christendom. Every Christian communion has its conservatives and its liberals, its charismatics and radicals and reactionaries. And the only mistake seems to be when anyone says, 'This way only!' or imagines that the truth lies in a dull average and compromise.

A long time ago I was shown the chapel at an American Air Force base. It was a chapel which had to serve everybody, and the problem was solved with typical American ingenuity: push one button and the lights came up on an altar simply furnished with bare cross; other buttons brought out candles in any permutation you wanted; another button and there was Our Lady bathed in a blue light; then rather like the cancel button on the organ everything disappeared and the chapel became a synagogue. But the thing which most cheered up the chaplain was the 'at rest' button. 'In a position of rest,' he said, 'we have a neutral altar!' And there was the bare altar with a Bible open at the twenty-third psalm; neutral, and useless to all concerned, the lowest common denominator, and a travesty of what unity is all about.

3 *That our joy may be complete*

For unity is about God, and his will. And God is infinitely great, beyond the comprehension of man, of immeasurable beauty and holiness. And we know him, not in different forms of truth, but in him who is the Truth, Jesus Christ. And like strangers at a party who seek a common acquaintance, we say to our fellow Christians of other traditions, 'So you know Jesus too! Any friend of Jesus is a friend of mine.'

And this is the spring of unity, and the spring of mission, for then we can say to the world together, in the words of today's epistle

What we have seen and heard we announce to you also, so that you will join with us in the fellowship that

we have with the Father and with his Son Jesus Christ.
We write this in order that our joy may be complete.

EPIPHANY 4

You are God's temple

1 Corinthians 3.10–17 (NEB)

1 Let each take care how he builds

Everyone was pleased when Rodney and Penelope fell in
love. They both enjoyed the popularity which comes with
good health and a clear skin and a thoughtful kindly
disposition.

They planned their marriage with care. On the day the
sun shone, the bells rang, and when on their return
Rodney carried his wife over the threshold he said, 'I will
love you for ever'. Penelope thought the same but didn't
actually say anything, being choked with emotion and
confetti. Their voices echoed a little, because stairs
without a carpet lend a certain resonance to a house.
'Never mind,' they said, 'we have two toast-racks, a card
over the mantelpiece which says, "God is the Unseen
Guest in this House"—and we have each other.'

It would be impossible to say when the estrangement
began. Indeed many of their friends would be surprised if
you suggested the marriage had failed, because in a way it
hasn't; it is as happy a partnership as exists behind many
of the tidy fronts of the houses in their road. Perhaps the
tidy little fronts had started the trouble, because Rodney
and Penelope gradually began to do what they had sworn
never to do—pay more attention to appearances than to
each other. And although voices wouldn't echo in their
hall now, they don't have much to say to each other that
could echo. Each has found new interests or revived old
ones, which while perfectly harmless in themselves

40

gradually come between them. Although they had pledged themselves to each other in the beginning, they are stealing back little parts of themselves. In a way it is a kind of theft.

We can understand our Lord's reaction to the commerce in the temple if we see God's relationship with his chosen people as a kind of marriage. The old prophets were always going on about it, and about the unfaithfulness of the people. The outward form of the marriage went on, and pillars of society would have been very shocked—they *were* very shocked—when it was suggested that the marriage had broken down. Even the commerce in the temple was not intrinsically wrong. There are the mechanics of religion to be performed. You don't make a home simply by expressing devotion to each other, the housework has to be done as well. So, if one expression of worship is to offer God sacrifices, there has to be provision for it, animals to be supplied, even a little man to sweep up the mess afterwards.

But what happened was that the mechanics of religion became ends in themselves, and somebody was making quite a good thing out of it. It was a kind of theft, not only of money, but of loyalty. And it all went on quite happily until our Lord appeared on the scene. He alters the whole scale of values, and ends and means get sorted out.

2 *The worth of each man's work*

We too have our mechanics of religion. We don't kill doves and lambs, though we do have our temple dues. We have everything that goes under the strange modern title of 'plant'—churches, organs, boilers, thuribles and bells—all of varying degrees of necessity; there is no virtue in being inefficient; we are here with work to do. So long as they remain our servants and do not steal attention from our Lord.

There are people whose religion never seems to get beyond the point of things. These are people who leave because someone else decorates their window. These are people who hold high office in the Church, and when they move to another town never go to Church again. They had stolen too much attention from our Lord for themselves. There are so many ways we can do it: we can be so convinced that we have the Gospel at our finger-tips that we confuse knowing about God with knowing God; we can be so insensitive to others that our very zeal foments discord in a congregation; we can divide youth from age with silly jealousies on both sides; our committees and organizations can become self-perpetuating, and such fringe activities that they don't help one person nearer God. The theft can be so gradual that we can lose God while still apparently about his work.

3 *The temple of God is holy*

If love is to be kept alive we must relate all we do to the person of Jesus. The man who claims that the Christian Gospel is simple is usually talking nonsense, but there *is* simplicity and directness at its heart. Jesus recalls us to basic loyalty, to seeing the wood for the trees, so that our worship may be a spring of mission—for we are here not only for God, but for others in the name of God.

In a few moments our Lord will be here, in the special way we know in this sacrament. The Lord will visit his temple, and those little fortresses which are our hearts. Have our affections become so alienated that he will greet us like thieves in his house of prayer? or are we too preoccupied to notice him, having forgotten what the temple is for, what we are for? Have we stolen back parts of ourselves until his coming seems an intrusion? Or is his a welcome step, so that we respond with love to his love? Once our Lord appears on the scene he alters the whole scale of values, and ends and means get sorted out.

Dear Lord, may we love you for ever.

EPIPHANY 5

The wisdom of the world

1 Corinthians 3.18–end (NEB)

1 *Standards of this passing age*

Notice has been received that from 1 July this district will be a 'Smokeless Zone'. This will please those of you who don't like incense! Accompanying the notice was an advertisement for 'Smokeless Fuel'. The advertisement was glossy, and gave the impression that if you heated your water by means of smokeless fuel the steam would part to reveal a pretty lady in your bath. I think I shall stick to gas. They can't help it, can they? They exploit the sexual element even in a lump of coke.

And now we have been hearing in the last week that Mary Magdalene became Mrs Jesus, and that their children were the first of a line of descendants alive to this day.

Those of you familiar with productions like *Jesus Christ Superstar* and *Godspell* will recall the dramatic difficulty caused by anyone quite so alluring as Mary Magdalene, in the presense of anyone so obviously *un*married as Jesus. 'I don't know how to love him,' she sang. Which was another way of saying that Andrew Lloyd Webber and Tim Rice didn't know what to do with someone who was, in the immortal words of my college lecturer, 'nothing but a harlot, pure and simple'.

It is so difficult for the purity of Christ to be comprehended by grubby little minds like ours. To the impure all things are impure. Since God invented it, marriage is good. But Jesus could give his heart to no individual if he was to be free to love us all.

2 *He traps the wise in their cunning*

If you have heard nothing about 'The Holy Blood and the Holy Grail' I apologize for mentioning it. But if you have

43

had it thrown in your face on the train to work you may have been tearing your hair out at this latest onslaught on all you hold dear. It is not a work of sound scholarship, and it requires far too much imagination to believe that the whole Christian faith is built upon falsehood and that the apostles died for a lie.

That the death of Jesus, the actual 'deadedness' of him, was faked or illusory, is not a new fancy. It is as old as Easter. 'The Chief Priests held a discussion with the elders,' St Matthew tells us in his gospel, ' . . . and they handed a considerable sum to the soldiers with these instructions: This is what you must say "His disciples came during the night and stole him away" . . . and to this day this is the story among the Jews.'

A Christ who did not die and rise again is a Christ who cannot save. And very soon in the history of the Church, when heretics were denying the true humanity of Jesus, and alleging that he was only pretending to be human and only pretending to die, the fact of his actual death had to be emphasized. This is why in a few moments we shall sing in the Creed, 'He suffered death and was buried'. Every word in the Creed which trips so lightly off our tongue marks a battlefield in which the truth was at some time defended. And none more than those words which proclaim Christ's humanity and divinity: 'God of the substance of the Father, begotten before the worlds, and Man of the substance of his Mother, born in the world.' This is a far cry from the picture of Jesus going to the South of France on a first century package tour.

3 *Folly in God's sight*

Why this sorry tale receives so much attention is that in hinting at secret knowledge and secret societies and hidden cults it appeals to that part of our nature which loves intrigue and mystery and being one-up on others. Secrets, passwords, rites only for those initiated into some secret knowledge—these have always been features of mystery religions and freemasonries and cults. I suppose they do no harm if the religious element is not taken seriously, or regarded as in some way superior to the simple love of Christ in his Church.

It needs to be stated with authority that in our dealings with God there is no secret knowledge, apart from the secret of his own heart as to why he should love us at all. For us to have to be admitted or groomed or indoctrinated or examined before God could love us is contrary to the way he deals with us. If we had to be clever in order to be saved, or if we had to be proficient in some brotherhood in order to be saved, or if we had to be good to be saved—what hope would we have?

It is a wonderful demonstration of God's love in dealing with us that on the one hand the study of his being can occupy the most brilliant intellect, and the expression of his glory can employ all the talents of wisdom and art; yet on the other hand he attracts the simple obedience and love of Bishop King's ploughboy, who when asked what preparation he would make for his Communion the next day replied that he would clean his boots and put them under his bed ready for the morning. If peasants are to be saved as well as professors it must be true that God has revealed himself not in esoteric knowledge or hidden riddles, but in the person of Jesus Christ, true God and true Man, ever to be worshipped and adored.

EPIPHANY 6

They have refused to honour him

Romans 1.18–25 (NEB)

1 *Misguided minds*

In one of the more famous Sherlock Holmes stories, the great detective baited the faithful but slow Watson with the remark: 'You have neglected the significant fact of the dog in the night-time.' 'But,' protested Watson, 'the dog did nothing in the night-time.' 'That,' said the infuriating Holmes, 'was the significant fact.'

There are many spheres of life where what does not happen is more important than what does. Very often I am asked to give a 'reference' for someone who is seeking a job, and I try to write good ones. But experienced writers, and readers, of references, are aware of a sort of code. The thing to look for is what is *not* said. A reference for a prospective bank clerk is eloquent in its silence if it says nothing about her integrity, but dwells long on the blueness of her eyes! Parents whose children get into trouble often say, 'I don't know why he did it, we've always given him everything he wants'—when it is what they haven't done that sticks out a mile. More marriages fail through neglect than through violence.

'We have left undone those things which we ought to have done.'

2 *They have bartered away the true God*

When we talk about 'sin', people imagine we are thinking of the most lurid things, but if we take the New Testament as our standpoint we see things differently. Our Lord was very tender to those in the thrall of the grosser sins, but there are many parables about failure: the man condemned because he had not made use of the talent entrusted to him; the foolish bridal attendants who had not made adequate preparation; the man at the wedding feast not wearing the right clothes (the point of that—because after all he had been swept in with no time to prepare—was that the wedding garments were provided by the host, and this man just hadn't bothered to pick his up). Then there is the dreadful picture of the last judgment 'Inasmuch as you have failed to do this and this, you have failed to do it to me'.

A picture is emerging here in which, if we are honest, we can see a good bit of ourselves. There are technical terms we can bandy about—we can talk about the 'mortal sin of sloth' (which is more than laziness—it is 'couldn't-care-less-ness'); we can talk about 'sins of omission'. The failures of love which God has to endure from us don't usually take the form of open hostility or opposition, though there are occasions when his will crosses ours and we sin with a high hand, choosing to do wrong. There is however something which wounds his heart no less, and that is the neglect or indifference, or the purely conventional churchmanship, which is our usual response to the love which blazes from the Cross. It is this lukewarmness which receives such condemnation in the Book of Revelation: 'I know your works, that you are neither cold nor hot . . . then I will spue you out of my mouth.' On our failures as well as on our wrong-doings we shall be judged.

Very often when someone has died one of the stages of bereavement is a great sense of remorse. It is not always for some wrong we have done the deceased in the past, but the opportunities for doing good that we have missed and which will never return.

So the very word for 'sin' in the New Testament is a word which describes an arrow missing its target. Sin is failing to be what we ought to be.

3 *Stifling the truth*

The great masters of the Christian life describe how there are three main stages in our growth towards God. There is the 'purgative way', in the early years of our discipleship, in which the most important thing is that we should be purged from the grosser appetites and sins. There is the 'illuminative way', in which these battles of our youth are overtaken by steady growth in knowledge and understanding. There is the 'unitive way', in which all our desires and longings have been drawn one way, to God. These are rough outlines, and the stages overlap. Each has its own particular temptation—to lust, to envy, to pride. But common to all are the sins of omission, the failure to be at each stage what we ought to be.

47

When we have done all, when we think we have God's approval, when we think we are better than other men, let us remember the significant fact of the dog in the nighttime. The dog did nothing. That is the significant fact.

NINTH SUNDAY BEFORE EASTER

Fools for Christ

1 Corinthians 4.8–13 (JB)

1 *Carnival*

There was a time when the court of no king was complete without its clown, its buffoon. He could get away with anything. He could interrupt, he could poke fun, he could ridicule, and yet be rewarded. I suppose the modern equivalent is the newspaper cartoonist, who always finds a ready sale for his original drawings amongst those he makes fun of most. We shouldn't think much of any politician who was offended by the impressions of Mike Yarwood. Indeed they themselves seem to become more and more caricatures of him.

It is for the same reason, I believe, that we have in our calendar not only an All Saints Day, but an All Fools Day too. The puncturing of pomposity, the cutting down to size, this is the other side of being human. Because men and women are not only animals who reflect and pray. We are also the only animals who laugh.

Within a rather sombre world comedians help to keep alive the spirit of carnival, or merriment, of fun bursting through. They serve society by feeding society's capacity to laugh at itself, the capacity to enjoy. Of course they are very serious people and take their work seriously, but, please God, they don't take themselves too seriously. They can't if they claim to inherit the spirit of carnival, for the very word carnival means a loosening of the reins, indulgence, cocking a snook (though I am not sure what a snook is, and perhaps you had better not tell me). They represent that other side of human nature, which has the capacity not only to laugh, but to laugh at itself.

2 *The spring of laughter*

What is laughter? Ask a scientist a silly question, and you get a silly answer: 'a laugh is an abrupt, strong expiration, followed by a series of expiratory-inspiratory microcycles superimposed upon the larger expiratory movements; the mouth is opened, the teeth are bared, and there is a generalized tremor, sometimes amounting to convulsion'.

But the spring of laughter lies in the contrast between dignity and the absurd: the banana skin, the temptation to giggle in church, the dustcart following the Lord Mayor's procession. 'Help, help,' cried the old lady (and this happened to me in the middle of a most solemn service in the cathedral). 'Help!' I was but a young priest, convinced that now my spiritual power had been instinctively recognized. 'Help,' she cried, 'my elastic has broken!'

St Paul who does not enjoy a reputation for merriment, sustains in the Epistle for today this passage of scornful amusement, using humour as the weapon to disarm his critics:

> *Here we are, fools for the sake of Christ, while you are the learned men in Christ; we have no power, but you are influential; you are celebrities, we are nobodies. . . . We are treated as the offal of the world, still to this day, the scum of the earth.*

3 *The dignity of man*

For those who help us to laugh we are grateful. They remind us that among the brutalities and trivialities of the world man is a creature who can laugh. Stephen Verney tried to photograph the degradation of Calcutta, 'but could not, because the open sewers were hidden by the laughing faces of children'.

Man laughs at the contrast between what he is and what

49

he might be, he laughs because absurdity is the other side of dignity. And the dignity of man lies in the purpose God has for him.

It is God's wish to share his life with us. And when in order to do this he entered his own creation, he did so in the person of Jesus. In the person of Jesus he took the very stuff of our humanity, and gave it a dignity above all else in creation. More than this, he gave us the capacity for joy—for joy, not the empty laughter of fools, but the deep joy which comes from the heart of God himself, for those prepared to be fools for the sake of Christ.

Learn to see this contrast in yourself, between what you are and what God wants you to be, and take that contrast very seriously indeed.

For when we come to church we put on our lips the most sublime expressions about God, and the most devout aspirations of faith. Because this does not always match your feelings you may think that you are a hypocrite. But this longing for God, this desire for holiness, has been placed in your heart by God himself, for without him you can never be satisfied.

The only reason for our existence is that God wants us to see him and be with him, and this contrast between what we are now, and what we shall be, is the biggest joke of all.

EIGHTH SUNDAY BEFORE EASTER

Is any cheerful?

James 5.13–16a (RSV)

1 *Cheerful in church*

I am sure we are meant to be cheerful in church, and not gloomy. 'Is any cheerful? Let him sing praise.' But I am talking of real happiness, and not that dreadful fixed grin which some Christians seem to adopt.

With new Christians we need to conspire so that church is a happy experience for them. But what one really wants them to possess is something more profound than happiness, and that is the capacity for JOY, for I am equally sure that we are meant to enJOY God.

Now I have been inhibited from preaching on joy ever since a sermon I once heard from a miserable old curate (no one you know!), who by some anatomical feat managed to grind his teeth on the word. It is always difficult to commend the Christian virtues lest you fall foul of the Trades Description Act.

But there is at the heart of all creation, because it belongs to the nature of God, a deep and abiding joy. 'Where were you,' asks Job, 'when the foundations of the earth were laid, the morning stars sang together, and all the sons of God shouted for joy?'

And that God should ask this question in the heart of a book like Job, which plumbs the depths of human suffering and depression, shows that we are dealing in Christian joy not with a facile optimism, but with a quality profound and fundamental for our very existence as children of God.

So it isn't surprising that the beauty of worship should give rise not only to happiness, but create in the depths of people's hearts that little tug of joy:

> *You have come to Mount Zion and the city of the living God, the heavenly Jerusalem,*
> *where millions of angels have gathered for the Festival with all the saints.*

2 The sign of sanctity

Now a saint is someone to whom God is so real that he makes God real to others. The Church has a process for recognizing saints and declaring them to be so. They have to pass a very searching inquiry into their conduct in this life and their intercession in the next. They are so diverse that there is no type of man, woman, boy or girl not represented in their ranks. But do you know what quality is invariably required before a person can be declared a saint? Whatever else is taken into account, the one thing each must have demonstrated in life is the spirit of joy. For you cannot make God real to others unless he is real to you, and if he is real to you there will be—underneath the pains and frustrations of life, behind its triviality and problems—there will be the spring of joy in your soul.

You know how over any place where the Queen is staying the Royal Standard flies ('There's the Queen,' the little boy said. 'That's the lady God saves'). Well, joy is the flag flown over the citadel of the heart to show that God is resident there.

There have been occasions in your life when you have felt this stab of joy. Its coming is independent of the weather or the state of your digestion, for it is a fruit of the Holy Spirit, and is a gift of God. But because you cannot grasp it, and dull routine closes round you again, you think it is an illusion. Far from it. It is at these moments that you are in touch with reality. When we come to worship God we grow to our full stature, and God will sometimes grasp us and give us joy. Is any cheerful? Let him sing praise.

3 Seized by God

Michel Quoist puts it in this way: 'The Christian who has "capitulated" to the Lord, who has said "Yes", often receives his reward immediately. The Lord gives him the joy of possessing him and of being possessed by him. Words are inadequate to describe this loving embrace of God. The boy who is "seized" by his Master right in the middle of the traffic, and has to dismount from his bicycle—suddenly unable to go on safely—will understand. So will the young girl who has to leave the workroom abruptly to hide from her companions her transfigured face.'

'I did enjoy that!' people sometimes remark after an act of worship, and then as typical English guilt descends, add

'but perhaps I shouldn't say that!' If it is only that you
have a liking for Victorian hymnody ('Let him sing praise'
does not necessarily imply Hymns A & M), or catching up
on the week's gossip, perhaps you shouldn't. But if God
has touched your heart and given you joy, what better
word than 'enjoy' can you use?

'Where were you when the foundations of the earth
were laid, the morning stars sang together, and all the
sons of God shouted for joy?'

Where were you?

You were already in the heart of God, for the very
purpose of your being is that you should enjoy God for
ever.

SEVENTH SUNDAY BEFORE EASTER

Not just a slave

Philemon 1–16 (TEV)

1 *My own son in Christ*

To those familiar only with the age of the motor car it may
be necessary to explain that 'blinkers' are the shields
placed to the side of horses' eyes to prevent their being
distracted or startled. So to call persons 'blinkered' is to
say that they can see in only one direction. It does seem,
looking at the long stretches of human history, that not
only horses and individual humans can be blinkered, but
whole generations. Each age seems to have its blind spots,
so obvious to us, but hidden then.

The calendar of the Alternative Service Book is
valuable in that it brings to our attention many of the
great social reformers—blinker-removers—of compara-
tively recent generations. Such was William Wilberforce,
who died in 1833 very soon after he had won the fight for
the abolition of slavery. For the first time in the history of

civilization the blinkers had at last been removed, and slavery was seen to be incompatible with the Gospel.

Even in the New Testament slavery is taken for granted, and Onesimus in today's Epistle is a slave. In the first century the Christian faith quite obviously took root at all levels of society, but in the first century slaves were merely urged to be good slaves, and masters merely urged to be good masters. The institution of slavery itself was not questioned. Yet the Gospel contained within itself the seeds of its dissolution, though it did take eighteen centuries for the seeds to grow and bear fruit.

2 *A brother in the Lord*

For fifteen years my eyes rested on one particular memorial on a church wall before its significance came to me. It commemorated a certain 'Captain of the Good Ship Ruby', who had been engaged for years, it said, 'in the Jamaica Trade'. And here his family, grown wealthy on the 'Jamaica Trade', had put this memorial to him in his parish church. But the Jamaica Trade was a three-cornered affair: rum to England, goods and guns to Africa slaves to Jamaica. They were good, honest, God-fearing people, but blinkered in that one respect of their attitude to slavery.

A more recent blinkering, but also at a safe distance from our consciences, I heard of from someone who had visited Johannesburg in South Africa at the time of the riots in the African township of Soweto. At the time of the worst upsets, he was with a white congregation who were praising God for the gifts of the Spirit, oblivious of the great social injustice within a few miles of them. Good, honest, God-fearing people, but blinkered.

3 *May God give you grace and peace*

It does seem as though in each generation God raises up prophet souls to puncture our complacency. With motes and beams to think about we are in no position to judge, and only a future generation will know what our particular blinkers are, within the Church as well as outside. We always hope that each generation will learn from what has gone before, so that enlightenment will advance with a kind of ratchet effect, unable to slip back into darkness. Sometimes people ask, 'Why is the world in such a mess after two thousand years of Christianity?' But besides answering, 'it might be still worse without it,' it is not strictly true to speak of 'two thousand years of Christianity', only of two thousand years of individuals who have responded or not to the love of God. Each child born is a fresh focus of self-centredness to be weaned into love of others for their own sake, and hence to a love of God. And all this besides the 'principalities and powers, the spiritual hosts of wickedness in the heavenly places'. It is a risk God takes to preserve our freewill. In a world of freewill men will be blinkered, they will abuse each other, disasters will happen.

On the London to Cambridge Road, the A10, just south of Ware, there is a small monument marking the spot where William Wilberforce lost his blinkers and came to his decision to fight the slave trade. The decision began a hard and long fight, won only a few days before his death. Actually the monument has had to be moved a few feet to one side to allow for the widening of the road. I like to think of this as an illustration of how the standpoint of one generation is by-passed by another.

Perhaps it is one of God's greatest kindnesses to us that he allows us at any one time to see only some small measure of how far we fall short of his glory.

LENT 1

Through fear of death

Hebrews 2.14–end (NEB)

1 *The same flesh and blood*

Long after unbelievers have stopped asking the Church for Baptism for their children, long after a church wedding is the thing to have, we shall continue to bury their dead. And I think the reasons for this are obvious: of all the 'rites of passage', that of death raises inescapably ultimate questions about life. What many people don't realize is that there is no legal obligation to have a funeral service at all. So long as the dead are disposed of within the requirements of the public health regulations you don't have to have any ceremony at all, let alone a religious one. It is however only the strong-minded atheist who writes such an understanding into his will.

The old Prayer Book, as you may have discovered in flicking over its pages during boring sermons, stipulated that the Church's funeral rites should not be used for any who had 'died unbaptized, or who had laid violent hands upon themselves'. We have a deeper understanding these days of what drives people to suicide, nor do we hesitate to express words of Christian hope over someone who for seventy years may have neglected all outward sign of Christian practice. Nowhere does the confusion seem greater between acting as a Christian priest, and acting as the local priest who happens to be Christian. There is of course all the difference in the world between the atmosphere of a Christian funeral, where the eternal issues are understood and where behind the grief there is a deep confidence in God, and a ceremony in which the eternal issues are obviously being reluctantly faced for the first time.

But let us ask a basic question: what is a funeral? It is, first of all, a dignified end to a body which has been the outward expression of a personality created in the image of God. Second, it is a vehicle for the grief of those who have been bereaved. The public acceptance of a death is a vital step in healing and restoration. Third, a funeral is something done for the dead. If you don't believe in praying for the dead you are left not with a funeral but with something little more than a 'bereavement service' for the mourners. We have all perhaps attended services like that, in which the rites of the Church have been displaced by a hotch-potch of prayers for the living and embarrassed praise of the dead. But if we have a sound grasp of the Church as a family spanning life and death, then we know our prayers for the dead are efficacious, prayers not only formalized in the words of the service, but prayers also which come from the unutterable grief of the heart.

2 *Those meeting their test now*

Let me say something here about the new rites of the Church, now included in the Alternative Service Book.

The charge is frequently made that the new services have been foisted by the clergy on an unwilling and resentful laity. Finding myself thus labelled as a revolutionary, when I thought I was a mild and aquiescent sort of chap, I have pondered why this should be. And I think that one reason why priests and laity look at things from different points of view concerns just this matter of the 'occasional offices'. Usually when people ask 'why did we have to change?' they are thinking of the Sunday Eucharist, whereas I am thinking of the tools of my daily trade which the occasional offices are. And I recall my relief when the new funeral rites were published, at a time when I was responsible for the conduct of over two hundred funerals a year. This was relief not only on behalf of instructed Christians, who are quite able to look after themselves, but relief on behalf of all those poor, lost, uninstructed mourners one tries to serve, whose only contact with the Church is at the turning points of life and death.

'Now the service we shall use', we can say to them, 'won't be a lengthy one—you don't want the whole thing dragged out—but it will say what you want it to say. You have told me all about the person who has died. We shall be able to thank God for all those good things you remember, so that we are not just mourning a death but thanking God for a life, and entrusting him into the care of the God who made him.'

3 *Their high priest before God*

I mentioned three things that a funeral does. There is a fourth: it is a proclamation of the Gospel. And the new rite moves confidently from a reminder of our own mortality (no pulling of the punches there), through thanksgiving, and finally to commendation.

If we think this is a prostitution of Christian rites on behalf of the ungodly, consider this: that as Christians we are not concerned with 'survival after death', but with resurrection—a definite act of God's love. To what degree of glory God assigns us at our resurrection is in his hands. No one comes to the Father except through Christ. *We* know Christ now, but he is the fulfilment of every religious longing which has ever stirred the heart of man since man began.

As I stand at the graveside, knowing that 'hell is paved with priests' skulls,' I think

> *'who for me be interceding, when the* just *are mercy needing?'*

LENT 2

Not every spirit

> *1 John 4.1–6 (JB)*

1 *The Spirit of God*

One of the questions which parents need to answer on the form of application for the baptism of their infants is whether or not they themselves have been confirmed. The same question faces those contemplating marriage. Sometimes, because they don't know what it means, they say, 'I'm not sure'. Then one can only point out that if they are not sure, then they haven't been. It can happen only as the result of a conscious decision on their part.

It is something like that with all that business about sin against the Holy Spirit, which has 'no forgiveness in this life or the next'. It is sometimes part of a morbid depression that people accuse themselves of having committed this sin. But it is not a sin you can slip into unawares, or by inadvertence. It is not a way God can catch you out when you are not looking. Just think: it is God the Holy Spirit who leads us into all truth. It is only if you grasp that truth, if you are grasped by God in all his beauty and power and love, and then deliberately refuse to accept that love, that you remain unforgiven; and then not because God refuses to forgive, but because you refuse to repent. This is how Christians can believe in the possibility of hell, of that final separation from God that hell is. We shall not find ourselves there through inadvertence, or by being caught out by God, but only if it is our deliberate choice.

But how could that be? How could we look at God and reject him? Perhaps habits of impenitence could grow so that we lose all capacity to repent, but we do not know. The Church has always rejoiced in proclaiming with great certainty that some people already share the joys of heaven, those whom we call saints, but the Church has never tried to identify the population of hell. The

59

Christian says, 'yes, I believe in the possibility of hell—that is the logical conclusion of God's great gift to us of freewill—but it is our prayer and hope that no one is ever finally in that state.' Certainly no one is there because of irritation on the part of God, or bad luck on the part of man.

2 The spirit of Antichrist

However, when all is said and done it remains as true today as ever it was that 'it is not against human enemies that we have to struggle but against the sovereignties and powers who originate the darkness of this world, the spiritual army of evil'. For if, as we believe, Jesus came not just to give us good advice or tell us moving stories, but to rescue us from the hell of separation from God, the conflict was and is real. The Church has a whole battery of armament to bring against evil deliberately welcomed and encouraged, but this is not deployed in the case of those who think they have been 'possessed' by devils against their will. It is a pity one has to go into this, but impressionable minds are constantly being assailed by films of the occult, and people imagine themselves to be possessed when they have only been frightened. Then in their distress they come and demand 'exorcism'. But this trivializes both evil and grace; it is a plea for 'white magic' to counteract the black.

3 One who is greater

We are the servants of a victorious Saviour, who tells us that 'all authority in heaven and earth is mine'. To begin to discuss exorcism or evil or the occult or any of the other nasty gropings of men's minds, without doing it in the knowledge and strength of Jesus triumphant and victorious, leads to captivity, to madness, to despair. So these fearful souls we try to steer away from this preoccupation with evil, because this bears its own fruit and springs from a morbid enslavement to self, and we try to lead them to the wholesome normalities of Christian life—to Baptism, to Communion, to fellowship, to the company of believers who are possessed by Christ. When Christ fills the heart there is room for nothing else.

It has been said that the possibility of hell is the greatest compliment which God could have paid his creatures, because it leaves the choice ultimately in our hands. What we need to remember is that we exercise this choice not in one final examination, but in the hundreds of choices which face us each day. The pattern of our lives is being woven as we live them, and in a hundred encounters and decisions each day we are deciding for God or against him.

Someone once asked me if I am thinking about God all day. To reply that 'being in the God business' I have no chance of doing anything else, would have failed to do justice to the depth of a real question. And to answer a straight 'no' would be misleading too. So I pointed out that everything she thought and did was coloured by the fact that she was a wife and mother. She couldn't always be conscious of her husband and children, but they were part of her, woven into the very fabric of her being, they helped to make her the sort of person she was. So surely it is with Christians. Our living and growing relationship with God is the unconscious assumption of our lives, which colours all that we do and decide and are. This is our armour against surprise attack. We are heirs of the kingdom, and the gates of hell shall not prevail against it.

LENT 3

Afflictions still to be endured

Colossians 1.24–end (NEB)

1 *The small cog*

In those rather murky days after the Second World War, when even I was recruited to the Forces, and the Royal Air Force paid me six shillings a day with keep (the 'keep' being mainly undercooked sausages), an officer cheered me up by saying that the sole reason for our training was that we might kill people better, and kill more of them. I hadn't really regarded myself as a killer, and had thought of myself more as a deterrent—the fact that I was there with my little screwdriver was surely enough to make any enemy think twice.

But the officer had at least succeeded in provoking thought, and in a way pointed to our human dilemma: the helplessness of the small cog in the vast machinery of world politics; the feeling that nothing we can do can make any difference; the sense of being tainted with the guilt of humanity. This is bad enough if you are not a Christian. But if it is your delight to serve the Prince of Peace, what does serving him mean in a mad world like ours? If all that is necessary for evil to prevail is for good men to do nothing, what in God's name can I do, who would be good?

2 *A point of exchange*

Well, let me ask another question first. Why is it that we are far more easily moved by the sight of one death than of millions? One battered child in England fills the papers for days. But our senses are numbed by the wholesale battering in some parts of the world. This reaction is well known by those who enlist our sympathy. The charities know that the picture of one starving child will bring in more money than the pictures of hundreds.

There are simple answers: that the agony is concentrated to a point which we can understand; that we can identify with a tragedy our minds can grasp. But there may be a clue here to our own individual worth in the whole work of God.

Newspapers make a great deal of the 'huge sum of human suffering', but this is quite an artificial idea: there is no 'sum of human suffering', there is just a huge number of humans suffering individually; 'the agony of a nation' is journalese, the agony of one man or one woman or one child is of an eternal dimension. And if this is true of the pain, may it not also be true of our response.

It was told of Saint Teresa that when she went to her bishop seeking permission to found her religious order, he—being a prudent man concerned for her welfare—asked her what her assets were. 'Fourpence' she replied. 'And what can Teresa do with fourpence?' 'Nothing,' came the answer, 'but a lot can be done by Teresa and fourpence and God.' What an awkward woman to deal with! But we can see that what she was offering God was a point of growth, a point of creation. A point, by definition, is apparently insignificant, but not if it is the moment of creation and the seed of growth.

3 God is creating now

For God is creating his world now. He didn't put the pieces together long ago, and wind it up, and leave it to run along. We exist only because we are in the mind of God now, and in his creative work we either co-operate or obstruct. And when we are met with evil we can react in different ways. We can meet it with more evil: we can retaliate; we can burst the fungus of wickedness so that its spores are broadcast and sow further evil. Or we can act like Christ and absorb the evil and offer good in return: love your enemies; do good to those who hate you. The Christian, if he is growing like Christ at all, is a point of exchange. You, little insignificant Christian, feel at a loss when confronted by the evil of the world. But the evil in the world consists just as much in the hatred, spite and filth you meet round the corner every day. If you offer yourself to God as this point of good for evil, God alone knows what infinite worth your action has.

> *It is now my happiness to suffer for you. This is my way of helping to complete, in my poor human flesh, the full tale of Christ's afflictions still to be endured, for the sake of his body, which is the Church.*

The only thing which has done any good in this world—in the sense of healing the disease rather than the symptoms, the only thing that has done any good has been the suffering and death of Christ. And I think that when we get to heaven we shall discover that the stage will be occupied not by those the world regards as famous, but by those who have offered God an opportunity for his love to grow.

We are here this morning in obedience to Christ's command to 'do this' in remembrance of him. Let us realize that we Christians use the word 'remember' in a special way, the opposite less of 'forget' than of 'dismember'. It is for us not just a recalling of the past. We are not recalling a dead Christ, but making present the living Jesus. This is our point of exchange. It is our privilege to re-member Christ to make him present in our own lives, and thus offer God a point through which his love and forgiveness many flow.

If all that is necessary for evil to prevail is for good men to do nothing, what in God's name can I do, who would be good?

'Do this!'

LENT 4

His veil was removed

2 Corinthians 3.4–end (TEV)

1 *Veiled souls*

At the last bazaar I bought a bulb in a pot. Knowing
where it came from I had no doubt that it would grow, but
I had strict instructions to keep it in the dark for three
weeks before I could expect anything to happen. Well, it's
happened, as you can see. From the tight little bulb there
emerged a tight little bud, and now this has opened up,
filling my study with its heady scent. A good fifteen
penn'orth if I may say so.

I have known lots of people like that bulb. When you
first meet them they are tight little knots of hesitancy and
shyness, closed in on themselves. But given the right
conditions they 'come out of themselves' as we say, and
blossom, and—not smell (you must allow the best
analogy to break down sooner or later)—but give off the
fragrance of friendliness and fun and openness. This is
why people seem to grow younger as you get to know
them. This is why shy people make the best actors,
because they are given a role to play which enables them
to express themselves.

To some extent we all play a role and hide behind it,
and I want to talk about Christian openness. This means
being open to each other at a greater depth of our being,
not being afraid to let people into our hearts and lives. I
speak with some diffidence here because it is not
something I find easy. Behind this fragrant exterior I am
but a small fluttering bird, and I have to learn the hard
way, like you.

Once a little boy, who lived in a long terrace of identical
houses, was asked the difference between his house and
all the others. 'It is the one,' he said, 'where I can go in
without knocking.' This is what a home is, isn't it?—a
place where you are accepted for what you are, and loved

for who you are, where the veil between people wears thin and it doesn't matter, where real person can meet real person.

If our life together in Christ means anything at all it should share this quality. The extroverts among us must be patient, and realize that their exuberance can be a screen to hide behind too. We introverts must not wait for people to knock on our door, but at least take it off the latch ready.

2 Their minds were closed

St Paul speaks of the veiled minds of the traditional Jews. He refers to the prayer shawls, as we would call them, to be seen to this day in any synagogue. He wants to unveil their hearts and minds to the light and love of Christ, for he knows the freedom which the Spirit brings.

There are moments in the history of mankind where a veil wears thin and we are in touch with reality. I mean the veil between our life, bound as we are by the finitude of space and time, between this and the eternal world. Such moments have been the great interventions by God in his saving acts.. At the birth of Jesus heaven over-flowed. Something happened at his baptism. This is described differently by the different writers—which is what you would expect from any evidence which had not been cooked—some speak of a voice from heaven, some of an assurance given to Jesus, some of a message to John the Baptist. But what all experienced was the thinning of the veil between time and eternity, a sense of openness between Jesus and his heavenly Father, a moment taken out of time, a moment when people were taken out of themselves and became open to greater truth, open to greater holiness, open to greater joy. At the empty tomb angels appeared.

Just as there are moments of time, so there are places too, where the veil wears thin. The Blessed Sacrament, the host placed in the palm of your hand, is a place and time in your life when you are in touch, literally, with reality. You have only to open your heart to sense it. In his writing on the chapel at Little Gidding T. S. Eliot speaks of it as a place 'where prayer has been valid'. We know the sense of holiness and the numinous possessed by some old churches and shrines.

3 *We have this hope*

I would say that if you want to be a good Christian in this frenzied world of ours, if indeed you want to retain your wholeness and sanity as a human being, you must seek out these moments and places where you can be in touch with reality. All the hesitations and reluctances which inhibit our dealings with each other have to be broken down too in our relationship with God. With him, above all, it is sinful folly not to be open. There are times and situations and places where this is easier and we should seek them out.

Some explorers were being guided by Indians through a South American jungle, and were disconcerted when their guides stopped for no apparent reason. Eventually they were able to explain: 'We are going too fast; we are waiting for our souls to catch up.' Make use of the quietness of the church, of the weekday Mass where the formality and bustle of Sunday gives way to the quiet intimacy of the spoken word and the stillness and lack of haste. Don't be afraid to contemplate going on retreat.

You will have had your moments and places where the veil has become almost transparent, I have had mine. I think you would agree that far from escaping from reality, these have been the most real moments of our lives. Nor is it something we seek instead of activity: more has been achieved in this world by those open to God than all the rest put together.

> *All of us, then, reflect the glory of the Lord with uncovered faces; and that same glory, coming from the Lord, who is the Spirit, transforms us into his likeness in an ever greater degree of glory.*

There is more in a bulb than meets the eye. There is more in us too, if only we will be open to God.

LENT 5

Captives in his triumphal procession

Colossians 2.8–15 (NEB)

1 *Do not let your minds be captured*

Getting back to the vicarage one day after assuring some poor soul that she was not haunted, I became aware of strange scuffling sounds, apparently in the wall, and in the room traces of soot, and on the air the smell of sulphur. Unlike those who are brave enough to watch the late-night films and therefore put an occult explanation on everything, and more like the other good housewives among you, I had an idea what the trouble was.

I pulled aside the gas fire, and into the room there fluttered a very black blackbird which had been trapped in the chimney. It had tried for hours to reach that little circle of light above it, which represented the only freedom it knew, whereas those outside the chimney knew its hope of rescue would come only when it was exhausted and fell to the bottom.

There are many people who at some stage of their life can recognize themselves in that blackbird, fluttering to get out from a threatening darkness, apparently abandoned and out of reach of help. This help can often only be given when the point of exhaustion has been reached, when they stop trying to fly high by their own efforts.

2 *You were buried with him*

It is fairly general Christian experience, and yours I am sure, that advances in the Christian life have come not from the times when we stride conquering through the world, but from the times of exhaustion and despair, when—at last—we allow ourselves to be accepted by Christ as we are, and not as we pretend we are. And to those sunk in depression, once all physical causes have been removed, it is the beginning of healing to know that however low they sink Christ is there before them—'My God, my God, why have you forsaken me?'

'If I go up to heaven thou art there,' says the Psalmist, 'and if I go down into hell thou art there also.' Christians who are depressed suffer a double burden—on top of their condition is the sense of guilt that they are denying their faith. Let Christ remove that too—there is no depth that he has not plumbed before them.

3 Alive with Christ

It is because of Christ's claim to set people free that Christians—when we live up to the name—are concerned whenever people are in any kind of bondage. And there are many kinds of that. Besides the psychological bondage we have just thought about there are all the limitations of physical handicap. There is the imprisonment of drugs. There is slavery to sin. We speak of the 'poverty trap'. There is the oppression of one person by another, the bullying of one class by another. There is actual physical imprisonment. I don't know how many of you have been to prison? Don't put up your hands now, but I have, in the course of duty. I recommend the experience to those quick to pronounce on law and order.

'I was in prison and you visited me.' You will remember those words from Jesus' terrifying picture of the last judgment. Some of you, I know, are involved in Amnesty International, concerned with Prisoners of Conscience throughout the world. The cleverer man becomes, the more sophisticated become his methods of manipulating minds and torturing bodies. 'All that is required for evil to prevail is for good men to do nothing.'

To bring Christ's freedom, God raises his champions and stirs consciences. But the skirmishes on the surface of human life are echoes of that deeper conflict with which we are concerned today, as we enter Passiontide. We watch with awe as the champion of champions carries the battle into the enemy camp. For of all bondages, the greatest is man's slavery to himself, when he lives apart from God.

> *On the cross Christ discarded the cosmic powers and authorities like a garment; he made a public spectacle of them and led them as captives in his triumphal procession.*

Defeated enemies trailed at the end of victory parades. Well to the fore of Christ's triumphal procession are those captive to his love, those who have allowed him to release them into the service which is perfect freedom.

PALM SUNDAY

Death on a cross

Philippians 2.5–11 (NEB)

1 *Bearing human likeness*

In these days of powerful bulldozers it is easy to clear a building site when you want to start building again. But in the days when you were limited to manual labour the best you could achieve was a rough levelling of the ground. This is why if you want to discover what happened in the past you have to dig down, because successive rebuildings gradually raise the level of inhabited sites. It is possible to visit Jerusalem and the rest of what is called the Holy Land, and see where all these things happened that we shall be thinking about this week. Often you have to rely on the work of archeologists, often you have to cope with the different outlook of the eastern mind, which likes to hide holy places under what we would call a litter of little lamps and shrines. If *we* had Calvary to display to the public, the Ministry of the Environment would go to great lengths to encourage grass to grow, so that it would always be the 'green hill'. But all you are allowed to do now is *touch* the top of the Calvary through a hole in the floor of the Church of the Holy Sepulchre—it is too holy to be exposed to the vulgar gaze.

I wonder if you realize how important it is that we should be able to visit the scene where Jesus did this and that, where he was crucified, where he appeared to his disciples alive again after the first Easter Day. It is because the Christian faith is not what we call a 'philosophy'—a theory worked out to try to explain the world we live in. No, the Christian faith results from certain historical facts, from certain things which God has done within human history, and in certain places on the earth's surface. These things are either historical facts or they are myths. If I didn't believe them to be facts I wouldn't be a Christian for another minute.

2 *Theatre and drama*

About this time of the year particularly many people revisit Jerusalem, and follow out again the events of those last days of our Lord's life on earth. If we can't go to Jerusalem these events are acted out in church—with our Palm Sunday procession, the watch of prayer from the Last Supper on Maundy Thursday to the Crucifixion on Good Friday, to the joy of Easter day with its 'joyful noise' and symbols of new life.

Don't be afraid at those words 'acted out'. To understand them we need to recover a distinction the ancient Greeks made between 'theatre' and 'drama'. We retain some of their meaning of 'theatre' when we use 'theatrical' in a pejorative sense—something artificial, a display, a show, something presented as a spectacle. But 'drama' is something which involves us to the depths of our being, which draws us into the story, so that it is *us* and *our* life which passes before us.

71

The events of Holy Week are in this sense *dramatic*. They involve us to the depths of our being because they reveal what human nature is like all the time. It has often been pointed out that we are the actors in this drama, that the men actually responsible for the execution were displaying no more that the sins and weaknesses men have always shared.

More important, however, is that these events reveal what *God* is like all the time. They happened once for all in human history—you can see the place where they happened. It is not without significance that we date our years 'AD', anno domini, year of our Lord. The events of which we speak are central to all human history. But there is an eternal dimension. The death of Jesus is more than a demonstration. It has changed the whole relationship of man to God for all time. We look back in history, but long after 'history' has ended we shall enjoy in eternity the fruits of what happened at that time and in that place.

> *Therefore God raised him to the heights and bestowed on him the name above all names, that at the name of Jesus every knee should bow—in heaven, on earth, and in the depths—and every tongue confess, 'Jesus Christ is Lord', to the glory of God the Father.*

EASTER DAY

Christ was raised to life

1 Corinthians 15.12–20 (NEB)

1 *What we proclaim*

Dotted here and there on the floor amongst the Easter vegetation are many little trays of what look like hors d'oeuvres, little things on sticks, left over from some holy cocktail party.

Take a closer look and you will see that they are miniature Easter gardens, made by the miniature people of our Family Service. You will be able to sense the care and imagination which have gone into them, and the pride with which they were brought to church on Good Friday. Quite a few local lawns are better without their moss, and look out for the Easter tomb with Lego doors which really open!

Now it is not necessary to salvation that you should be able to make an Easter garden, showing three crosses on the green hill, and the empty tomb with the stone rolled away, and the Lego doors open. But it is necessary to our salvation that there should be something to make a model of. For in matters of the Christian faith we are not inventing comforting fables, but dealing with facts, and things that God has done—so precise that you can visit the places where he has done them, and make models of the background to the events, even if Lego doors do represent a variant tradition!

At Easter we proclaim the fact of the Resurrection, and Sunday is for ever the holy day of Christians, the Lord's day, for it was on Sunday, the first day of the week, that Jesus was raised from the dead.

> *If Christ was not raised, then our gospel is null and void.*

2 *Witnesses to the resurrection*

So, just as children have grubbed about with stones and moss and flowers and clay, it is good for us at one stage of our discipleship to realize how down-to-earth God is.

Yet the disciples were directed away from the empty tomb, and so do we need to move on in our discipleship. We need to realize that what transformed the disciples from defeated men to triumphant apostles was not so much an empty grave as the living experience of the living

73

Jesus. Ask them what they meant by the Resurrection and they would speak not of graves but of Christ. And so it has been through the ages: each generation discovering afresh and at first hand that Jesus lives, and lives in their lives; and experiencing a growing response to a Christ who holds us in his heart and shows himself alive to us in so many ways.

We are here today because to each of us Jesus is real, Jesus is present, and God makes himself known to us in him. No wonder we make a '*joyful noise*' and sing Alleluia fifty-seven times (you might just check that for me). Alleluia means 'Praise God' and is a sort of holy hooray!

3 *Christ's resurrection and ours*

We are the Easter people, and we are concerned not just with Christ's Resurrection but ours as well. This new life is marked ritually in our Baptism. In this, as Christ died and rose again, so do we die to our old nature and are born again. This is why we renew our baptismal vows at Easter.

Our resurrection is also the hope to which we look forward after our own actual death. Resurrection, like all life, is the gift of God, is completely dependent on him, and nothing that we can earn or deserve.

> *If it is for this life only that Christ has given us hope, we of all men are most to be pitied.*

But all Christians are poised somewhere between these two events, our Baptism and our death, the distance being more precisely known in one direction than the other. None of us is in an Alleluia-ish mood all the time, and we shrink rather from those Christians who pretend that they are. Our lives run down. They get flat. The very gifts of God become commonplace, our marriages become stale, and hope dies. Christians feel doubly guilty when they experience these things. They despair of themselves and in consequence despair of God. Our sins become so familiar to us that we can't imagine ourselves without them. We begin to doubt if life can ever be different. The light of our life, and our sense of God, is extinguished, and we are as good as dead.

Our dear Lord wants you to know that resurrection is not just an event in the past or a hope for the future. From these little deaths God can raise you to new life NOW! Man and wife, dead to each other, cannot summon up more than the polite pretence of life, but God can raise the dead! Prayer dries up on us, the sacraments become dull, the progress of ritual and ceremony bores us. But God can raise the dead!

Look back on your life, and realize how often things have had to die: your plans; your ideas. These had to die before God could raise new life—not restore the old in dull continuation, but create something new and unimaginable.

We see this not only in individual lives, but in the Church herself. Cherished attitudes and cherished possessions have had to die before God could create new life.

Don't be afraid, God is in the resurrection business. Expect to be surprised by him!

EASTER 1

The assayer's fire

1 Peter 1.3–9 (NEB)

1 *Gold standard*

Mrs Silsby struggled upstairs on her arthritic legs into her cold bedroom on pension day and secreted another pound note in her mattress. One of the pathetic things about Mrs Silsby and so many people who save for a rainy day, is that she failed to recognize the rainy day when it came, and another pound a week spent on fuel would have saved her from the pneumonia which overtook her a few weeks later. But one of the pathetic things quite outside her control was that the pound she put aside last year was worth less now. Mrs Silsby is now in paradise, where the market value of sterling is irrelevant.

There are people still alive who remember when every banknote represented gold held by the Bank of England, and what it still says on the note is, 'I promise to pay the bearer on demand the sum of one pound'. It is a very unwise government which simply goes on printing money. Unless it bears some relation to true wealth we are overtaken by inflation.

2 *Spiritual inflation*

In the Christian life we have certain things which are of value in themselves, and others which are valuable only if they bear some relation to this real wealth. The one thing needful is a living relationship with God. This closeness to God is our true wealth, our gold standard. The things which the man in the street regards as particularly Christian—being kind, being honest, being pure, being patient and so on—must bear some relationship to the true wealth within, or whatever value they have is soon lost, we suffer from spiritual inflation. It is a matter of experience that unless our moral standard springs from love of God, it declines, for individuals and for nations. Next time you hear people advocating the teaching of ethics, or rules of behaviour, as a substitute for the Christian faith, walk round this enormous stranded cart and you will see they have left the horse behind.

Parish organizations come under the same judgment. Pastoral wisdom determines that these should be 'open-ended'—but not at both ends! Or people will pass through them and never come in touch with the heart of the matter. The further we get away from Christ, the further are we getting from the point.

3 *The individual*

This search for a standard is tied up very closely with our

search for our true selves. A girl in a retreat I once conducted put this very clearly when she said, 'When I am here in the convent I am one person, but I am another person at school, and yet another person at home. Which is the real me?' We must have had a remarkably smooth upbringing if that doesn't ring a bell in us. Is it indeed yet a thing of the past? The front we present to the world represents a reasonably consistent person, but we know that this is often only a façade.

But we should find as we grow spiritually more mature that we do grow spiritually more consistent. We cease to be blown about by every wind of doctrine, as St Paul says, and the craftiness of men, as we grow up into Christ. The more spiritually mature a man is, the more integrated he is. This is why great men are essentially simple people in the sense not of shallowness but of consistency; their outward selves match more and more accurately the inner selves; their lives are on the gold standard; their lives conform more and more to Christ, which by another of those Christian paradoxes, does not mean becoming more and more like one another, but each more and more gloriously himself.

> *Even gold passes through the assayer's fire, and more precious than perishable gold is faith which has stood the test.*
> *You have not seen Christ, yet you love him; and trusting in him now without seeing him, you are transported with a joy too great for words, while you reap the harvest of your faith, that is, salvation for your souls.*

EASTER 2

The wedding supper

Revelation 19.6–9 (NEB)

1 *First Communion*

We are familiar with the way in which the Church's year presents to us first this, and then that, aspect of Christian life, how the mood changes from season to season. It is not so long since we were being rather solemn during Lent and Holy Week. Now we are within Eastertide, and today's New Testament reading gives us a glimpse of the worship of heaven:

> *Alleluia! The Lord our God, sovereign over all, has entered on his reign! Exult and shout for joy and do him homage, for the wedding-day of the Lamb has come!*

But then the Christian life is like that all the time—at its heart a deep earnestness and simplicity, but springing up always into joy and light and celebration.

To those of you beginning your communicant life this morning let me strike the note of great simplicity.

Through all the strangeness of doing a new thing for the first time, and the wondering if you are doing the right thing and are in the right place at the right time—through all these superficial worries, cling to the simple truth, that Jesus is present in this sacrament in a special way. Before he returned to heaven he made this promise to his Church: 'I will be with you always.' Jesus keeps his promises, and nowhere does he more fundamentally fulfil this one than here.

> *Happy are those who are invited to the wedding-supper of the Lamb.*

Inscribed on the bread as it is put into your hand you will see the Lamb of God—a poetic way of describing Jesus not as a pale memory of some figure in the past, but as he is: alive, glorious, the same yesterday and today and for ever, holding you in his heart and mind now, as you have always been in the heart of God.

2 The God of heaven

Alleluia! The Lord our God, sovereign over all, has entered on his reign!

Now I am very conscious that in much of our preparation for Confirmation and Communion we have talked a lot about what I would call 'churchy' things. And this vision of the joy of heaven is a reminder of our destiny, of why God has made us. A great deal else has happened too, of course. You know how this group has grown together, and how the first strangeness and guardedness have disappeared and a genuine friendship has grown up. This always happens when people meet in the name of Christ; it is another way he keeps his promise: 'Where two or three are gathered together in my name, there am I.' But what we must never imagine is that in the Church we wind ourselves into a kind of cocoon, secure from outside pressures and difficulties, turning our backs on the world. No, in Jesus God comes to live in his world, and we must learn to recognize him everywhere. Because we have known him in fellowship and because we have known him in Communion, we shall the more easily recognize him elsewhere.

3 The God of earth

Let me show you what I mean by telling you of a very great man, Frank Weston, Bishop of Zanzibar. The name will strike a chord in some hearts, but since what I am talking about happened half a century ago, not all hearts are old enough to have this particular chord struck in them. Frank Weston fought hard for the Eucharist, and no one fought more effectively. It is difficult for us to imagine what a great battle had to be fought in the Church at that time to have it taken for granted as the centre of our worship, and to have the real presence of Jesus in the sacrament acknowledged and worshipped. The climax of the victory was marked by a great Congress in the Albert Hall (in Kensington, not Zanzibar), and undoubtedly he dominated the huge gathering.

No one was surprised when he exclaimed, 'I beg you brethren, not to yield one inch to those who would for any reason or specious excuse deprive you of the Sacrament. . . . I want you to make your stand for this not for your own sakes but for the sake of truth first, and in the second place for the sake of reunion hereafter.'

But his last word was this: 'You cannot claim to worship Jesus in the Sacrament unless you pity Jesus in the slum. Go out into the highways and hedges, go out and look for Jesus in the ragged and the naked, the oppressed and the sweated . . . look for Jesus, and when you see him gird yourself with his towel and wash his feet.'

> *His bride has made herself ready, and for her dress she has been given fine linen, clean and shining. (Now the fine linen signifies the righteous deeds of God's people.)*

Wherever you go, to home, to school or work, look for Jesus in the eyes of other people. Because those eyes will now be looking at you, in order to see Jesus. A Christian is a marked person, and their only chance of seeing Jesus may be when they meet you. If you faithfully keep company with him, it is him they will see.

EASTER 3

The gospel that I preached

1 Corinthians 15.1–11 (NEB)

1 *Jesus was raised to life*

The parable about Dives and Lazarus *is* a parable, and not a precise account of our destiny in the next life—all that about Abraham's rather hairy bosom is not everyone's idea of bliss, not Queen Victoria's for instance. In mourning one day for one of her many relatives, swathed in crêpe and driving in an open carriage called a sociable, she was so silent that her lady-in-waiting thought it time to make a little conversation. 'Oh your majesty, think of when we shall see our dear ones in heaven.' 'Yes,' said the Queen. 'We will all meet in Abraham's bosom,' said the lady-in-waiting. 'The Queen will *not* meet Abraham,' said the Queen.

No, the parable of Dives and Lazarus is not about bosoms, nor an excuse to tell stories about Queen Victoria. It is about the nature of belief and the place of proof: 'if they will not listen either to Moses or the prophets, they will not be convinced even if someone should rise from the dead'.

Belief in God always requires a leap of faith. Conviction and commitment are larger than intellectual assent. What God requires is not submission at the end of an argument, but love freely returned. There is a part of us, of course, which would like arguments for the Christian faith so convincing that we could hit our opponents over the head with them. But we will never be given those arguments, nor for that matter will our opponents ever have such arguments to return. What God requires is not submission at the end of an argument, but love freely returned.

There is a part of me still to be redeemed that feels I could have made a more convincing job of the publicity for the Resurrection: I would have had Jesus appearing to the High Priest and saying 'So there!' But no, Jesus appears only to those who already love him, and to those who, however surprised, can only respond with love and say, 'Of course—it had to be like that!'

You will recall how what is known as the Turin Shroud is held by some to be the touchstone of belief in the Resurrection. This is the cloth which may be the actual burial cloth of Jesus after his crucifixion, with an impression of his features so remarkably implanted that only some burst of energy unknown to man could have produced it. You know how moving the scientific inquiry is, how it edges us towards the belief that we are in touch here with something that has been in touch with Jesus. It may be that science will so clear the decks that we shall be able to say, 'This could indeed have been the shroud of Jesus dead, and the veil through which rose Jesus alive and glorious.'

But two qualifications need to be made. First, if it could be proved it might reinforce our belief and wonder, but it could not change the nature of our belief. Our faith in Christ alive and glorious does not depend on this one thing, for if it were disproved the nature of our faith would not change either. Secondly, it would not lead to conviction on the part of the general public and the beating of many feet to the doors of the Church. For their disbelief is not of that kind, their failure to respond to the love of God is not a suspension of belief about things: they will not be convinced even if someone should rise from the dead.

Religious belief is often accompanied by a fascination in relics. There are many supposed relics of the Cross on which Jesus died, there are many relics of the saints. These relics, rightly used, have been an aid to faith and devotion, and wrongly used have led to superstition and abuse. It has been left to a scientific age to find scientific fascination in the relic which the Turin Shroud might well be. Rightly used it can be an aid to faith and devotion, and wrongly used lead to superstition and abuse. But of itself it will only aid belief, it will not of itself bring a man to say, 'I turn to Christ!'

3 *In the end he appeared even to me*

No doubt you wonder at times about the mystery of why some people are overwhelmed by the love of God, while others live their lives apparently oblivious. There seems to be this dividing line between those who are aware of the eternal, aware that we live our lives against the background of something or someone profoundly greater and other than ourselves, and those who apparently never raise their eyes above the current thing or the present concern. The time when I wonder about these things is as I wander round the parish, and go down whole roads where I may over the years have been in only one home. I reflect on how lightly we touch this vast population. We touch it more than we think, of course: we bury their dead and marry their daughters and educate some of their children; but how is it that they suffer this spiritual handicap and are blind to what we see so clearly?

And then, equally inexplicably, the Confirmation class fills up. No one has argued them into coming. It is simply that in some way God has laid his hand on them, and, far from beating them with argument, has attracted them with love. No arguments, no 'proof', but an attraction greater than all other. Relics and miracles convince the convinced; they do not command belief, because God will never command our love.

Among Chaucer's Canterbury pilgrims there was a purveyor of relics, relics scornfully referred to by Chaucer as 'pigges bones'; and there is also the humble parish priest who 'taught Christ's law and first he followed it himself'. We are left in no doubt of the religious worth of the two men, nor of the worth of what they purveyed.

83

One sold his proof for money, the other lived his proof for nothing.

For in the end it is not things which make God believable, nor imprints on Turin shrouds; it is Christians, who bear the imprint of the risen Christ, and are so radiant with his love that in them the very features of Christ himself become visible.

EASTER 4

On the island of Patmos

Revelation 3.14–end (RSV)

1 *To the seven churches*

It was the first day of the week, a Sunday. The old Archbishop was beginning to feel his age, but in spite of his rheumatic twinges he was drawn yet again to his vantage point, on the top of the cliffs of the island on which he would now live out his days in exile. As his dim eyes looked out over the rocky coast towards the mainland, his heart went out to the seven dioceses there for which he was responsible before God.

As it was Sunday, he knew that the members of his Christian family would be meeting in secret places and caves and behind locked doors for their Eucharist together.

They would be meeting in secret because this was the first century AD, when it took a brave man to be a Christian, as it still does in many parts of the world today.

And the old Archbishop trembled when he thought of their weaknesses, and the fresh persecutions in store for them.

And as he thought of them, his thoughts passed into visions; he saw their Eucharist merge into the heavenly Eucharist, where our Lord eternally offers his perfect sacrifice, and he was commanded to write to them the message of God himself.

These letters we can still read, in the first three chapters of the Revelation of St John the Divine, and one of them is our reading today:

> *From John to the seven churches of Asia, Grace and peace to you from him who is, who was, and is to come . . . from Jesus Christ . . . the first born from the dead, the ruler of the kings of the earth.*

And then there follow the messages to each of the seven Churches.

2 *God knows us*

To this church write

> *Here is the message of the first and the last, who was dead and has come to life again. I know your works, how hard you work, and how much you put up with . . . nevertheless I have this complaint to make: you have less love now than you used to.*

And to this church write

> *Here is the message of the Son of God. I know your works and how charitable you are . . . nevertheless I have a complaint to make.*

Through each of the letters there runs like a solemn refrain

> *I know your works, I know all about you.*

Why did those Christians of the first century need to be reminded of anything so obvious as that God knew them through and through?

Because, like us, they were quite capable of shielding

themselves from the obvious. We erect round us a barrier of habit and convention which screens the truth about us from our neighbours (and from ourselves) and we think it fools God.

> *O Lord thou hast searched me out and known me, thou understandest my thoughts long before, thou art about my path and about my bed, and spiest out all my ways.*
>
> *(Psalm 139)*

Even the faith and charity of the seven churches did not spare them, when God saw some tampering with the faith, or some compromise with evil:

> *you are neither cold nor hot. Would that you were cold or hot! So, because you are lukewarm, I will spew you out of my mouth.*

God knows all about us, and the secrets of our hearts. He sees behind our outward behaviour to our true motives. He knows what only he and we can know—whether we are sincere in our prayers and generous with our giving or casual about our communion. He sees through all excuses. Special pleading and sailing as close to the wind as possible are no good. He demands the whole of us, and not just the part left over from other attractions, and he will be satisfied with nothing less. He knows if our frenzy of good works is just another way of hiding from him. He pursues us, he will give us no rest, he will never let us go.

'How often,' cried George Tyrrell, 'have I tried to throw the whole thing up, but always that strange young man on his cross drives me back again!'

What tyranny is this? Why won't God leave us alone?

3 *God loves us*

Because, madness of all madnesses: because he loves us.

He knows all about us, and the secrets of our hearts, yet he loves us. Because the greatest secret of our heart is the one he planted there himself. This is the desire for him—this better part of ourselves which wants to love and serve him—this desire which has brought us here this morning.

I know your works

There is no need to be afraid in coming to one who loves us so much.

I know all about you

There is no need to be ashamed in coming to one who loves us so much. If we are afraid to make our confession he already knows why—we can't shock God.

God pursues us with love, because his delight in having made us prevails even over our lack of love, because we don't really love God very much.

Conclusion

And so the old Archbishop was also commanded to write, as we have already heard this morning

> *Those whom I love, I reprove and chasten; so be zealous and repent. Behold, I stand at the door and knock; if any one hears my voice and opens the door, I will come in to him and eat with him, and he with me. He who conquers, I will grant him to sit with me on my throne, as I myself conquered and sat down with my Father on his throne.*
> *He who has an ear, let him hear what the Spirit says to the churches.*

EASTER 5

Going to the Father

1 Corinthians 15.21–28 (RSV)

1 *God is everywhere*

There was actually a time, before television, when it was possible for public people to live private lives. The Duke of Windsor, whom the mature among us remember as the last Prince of Wales, used to say that he could walk the streets of London unrecognized and unacclaimed—contrast that with the coverage of Royalty today!

It is difficult to look back from our electronic age and imagine a time when famous people were not also familiar. When the Pope was in hospital we even had a picture of the Pope in bed—my goodness!

To go into any kind of 'showbiz' these days means deliberately accepting that you will from that moment be instantly recognizable: Angela Rippon no doubt has her privacy, but it is not on the streets of England, for the men in the streets would point and stare.

But this ubiquity—being everywhere—is one-sided: we can recognize Morecambe and Wise, but they do not know us from Adam and Eve, apart from what we are wearing. When I see someone I know on television, I want to tap the screen and say 'Hello!', but that fantasy only underlines my point.

Now God is ubiquitous—God is everywhere—and he has been doing it from long before man invented the cathode-ray tube. God, we say, is above all things, and outside all things; he is wholly other than things, for he created all that is. There is no gap greater than that between creation and the creator.

And when we talk like this we are describing God's TRANSCENDANCE. God, we say, is transcendant, outside us, above us.

2 *God within us*

But this is only part of the truth. I look into things and recognize God there too; I look into myself, into that heart of hearts completely private and shut off from every other human being, and I discover God there. I cannot exist, nothing can exist, unless God is in it.

And when we talk like this we are describing God's IMMANENCE.

He is both TRANSCENDENT and IMMANENT, other than his creation, yet its very breath.

3 *The Ascension of Jesus*

Now look at Jesus.

In him we see God entering his creation in a unique way. St Paul says that in becoming man he 'emptied himself', and whatever we may understand about that, we see at a glance that his earthly life was a very limited and limiting experience. We can travel further in an hour than Jesus travelled in the whole of his lifetime. Although we hear of crowds round him, they are few compared with the many million who heard the Archbishop's sermon at the royal wedding. The numbers who could in the course of one human life meet the Son of God, touch him, hear him, see him, are a minute fraction of all the men and women who shall ever live. Even at his arrest he had to be identified by an intimate friend, not even an identikit picture was available to the temple police. How was Jesus to be ubiquitous, present to all men at all times?

What God did was to exalt Jesus to his right hand in heaven (such is the language we are forced to use): Christ ascended up on high, so that he might be present to all men. Instead of being limited to the human acquaintance of one human life, he would now be available to men without limitation at all; instead of being limited to one age and culture, by entering eternity he could be present to all times.

Christ ascended up on high that he might fill all things.

And unlike my feeble attempt to tap the television screen and say 'Hello', this eternal presence of Christ is not one-sided. If I recognize Christ and greet him, it is because he already knows me. He is wholly other, yet I am in him, because it is one humanity we share. He is the friend beside me, behind me, round me; he is the person with me, he is my partner in my work, in my marriage, in my home; where two or three are gathered in his name, he is HERE—lovingly greeting and lovingly greeted.

And so in today's Epistle St Paul says,

> *When all things are subjected to him, then the Son himself will also be subjected to him who put all things under him, that God may be everything to everyone.*

It is our Christian experience that the unknown has been made knowable by God in Christ; that at the heart of all existence, because in the very heart of God, is *our* human nature, raised to such a dignity that even the angels wonder.

4 *Ascension Day*

It is this wonder that we celebrate on Thurday, Ascension Day. I am sure that you heard this called a 'holy day of obligation'. But if we talk of obligation, this is my obligation to you, dear Lord: not from some discipline imposed from without, but that you love me without desert, for you are closer than a brother, you are in me and with me.

But, my dear Lord Christ, you transcend all that is, for of all things you are Lord and King.

Though you are risen, ascended, glorified, may I know as I am known, and may I be lost in wonder, love and praise.

So, in the words of the young man concluding a letter to

90

his beloved, a letter of utmost love and promise of everlasting devotion:

P.S. See you Thursday, if it's not raining.

SUNDAY AFTER ASCENSION DAY

Lord of all creation

Ephesians 1.15–end (TEV)

1 *Human and divine*

If you are fortunate enough to be in Jerusalem itself, you begin the Stations of the Cross at the very point where the exchange between Christ and Pilate took place: 'You are a king then.' 'It is you who say it.' 'Yes I am a king. I was born for this. I came into the world for this.'

Today a convent stands over the place where Pontius Pilate had his barracks. The sisters of the convent lead you down to the very stones of the very courtyard. After all, you go to the Holy Land to stand where Christ stood, but this is too close for comfort. And you push your way out into the narrow streets, following the traditional Way of the Cross, until you reach Calvary and the Tomb, in the Church of the Holy Sepulchre.

It is a rubbing of one's nose, psychologically and emotionally, in the human drama of that original journey of Christ with his cross, 'olfactorily' as well (if there is such a word) for there is nothing piously discreet about the smell of such a crowd on a hot day.

The execution of Christ the King is a drama which man has never been able to ignore. But you will have noticed how in representing it in art, and music, and drama, there is a constant swing in emphasis between the human aspect of it, and the divine. Our small human minds, limited as they are by time and space, find it difficult to comprehend the whole.

2 *Christ the king*

We have lived in a generation now which for some years has concentrated on the humanity of Jesus, 'The Man for Others', the 'Brother of Mankind'. Other ages, and other cultures (notably the Eastern Orthodox icon tradition) have concentrated on the divine nature, Christ the Lord of all creation. One reason, I think, that Graham Sutherland's tapestry of Christ in Coventry Cathedral is not instantly popular is that a stern Christ in majesty is not a popular figure in an egalitarian age. You know how crucifixes reflect the same dichotomy: one will show a blood-soaked, suffering Christ; one a Christ crowned, reigning from the tree.

Now we are experienced enough in Christian affairs to know that we do not have to choose. Both these expressions are true. Christian truth lies far more in the realm of paradox, of holding apparently conflicting views in balance, than in the realm of the dull average. So we know the Jesus of Good Friday and the Jesus of Ascensiontide, and our way to worship him in the spendour of heaven lies through this sacrament of his Body and Blood.

3 *The king and the kingdom*

The Church is in danger only if she confuses Christ's triumph with earthly triumphalism. For the hand which holds the sceptre is a wounded hand, and the feet we fall before bear the mark of nails.

How will Penzance become more and more the Kingdom of God? Penzance for Christ! Christ the King of Penzance!

Such acquaintance as we have with the ways of God would not lead us to believe such a victory would be won with the takeover of the town by a triumphalist Parochial Church Council, beating all opposition into subjection. Let me paint you another picture.

If you have ever flown in an aeroplane by night, you will know the fascination of seeing the lights of towns below, and if you know the towns well you can recognize them from the pattern of lights of streets and industries. It is even more moving when you fly over, say, vast tracts of Africa by night, where there is no industry, no streets to be lit. And then to see, here and there, isolated specks of light. And you know that below in all that darkness there is a fellow human being, living, breathing, hoping.

So does God look down on to the darkness of this town, to see his love shining back to him from all the hearts he has touched. I think that if we were to see this with God's eyes we should be surprised by the extent of his kingdom. There would be the obvious brilliancy, of course, of the Blessed Sacrament, and the lesser constellations of those who openly acknowledge Christ because we know and try to love him. But there would be many points of light in surprising places, as Bishop Michael Ramsey reminds us: 'Don't let us ever doubt that God is present in human lives, working perhaps at inaudible levels in the experience of men and women. We must never carry the Christian Gospel to people without reverencing the divine image in them, and we must be ready for the unexpected and unlikely to happen in terms of the presence of God in them.'

> *God put all things under Christ's feet and gave him to the Church as supreme Lord over all things. The Church is Christ's body, the completion of him who himself completes all things everywhere.*

You, Christ, are the King of Glory, the eternal Son of the Father.

When you became man to set us free, you did not abhor the Virgin's womb.

You overcame the sting of death and opened the kingdom of heaven to all believers.

You are seated at God's right hand in glory. We believe that you will come, and be our judge.

Come then, Lord, and help your people, bought with the price of your own blood, and bring us with your saints to glory everlasting.

PENTECOST

The mighty works of God

Acts 2.1–11 (RSV)

1 *Elemental forces*

Although this is the day of wind and fire, consider for a moment the many aspects under which we encounter the substance of water. Water is so fundamental to our existence on this planet that we have a mystical relationship with it. Soon we shall be sitting on the beach and throwing stones at the sea. The sea dwarfs us by its immensity and power and the relentlessness of its tides. Yet the tides can be predicted to a minute and an inch. We will travel miles to see a waterfall, yet will harness it so that it will drive our machines and generate our electricity. We will pipe it to our homes. It cleanses and gives life. But it is also inside us: seventy per cent of us is water. Although without it we should cease to exist we take it completely for granted.

Today is the festival of God the Holy Spirit. In the reading from the Acts of the Apostles we heard again how he poured upon the early Church like a great waterfall, in a demonstration of wonder and power, overwhelming them with such an awareness of God that they were transformed. The day it happened was the Jewish feast of Pentecost, and this is why we refer to this experience as pentecostal. There have been many times in the history of the Church when this kind of experience has been renewed, and there are Pentecostalist Churches which keep the experience alive. Some Christians today speak with tongues, as did the Apostles. It is not so much ecstatic uncontrolled utterance, as a language of liberation and praise. Where this movement is genuinely of the Spirit it brings joy and peace and assurance. It errs only if it says this is the only authentic experience for Christians. For just as water is most productive and fruitful when it is channelled and directed, so can God the Holy Spirit work through order and discipline within the Church, and God the Holy Spirit is present just as much in the normalities of Christian life.

2 *Gifts of the Spirit*

We know the presence of the Spirit by his signs: where we see growth and joy in Christian souls—there, we say, is God the Holy Spirit at work; where we see the Church stumbling towards unity and mutual love—there, we say, is God the Holy Spirit at work; where we meet men of goodwill in the world, whether they are Christians or not—there, we say, is God the Holy Spirit at work.

For God the Holy Spirit is within us and part of our being, and without him our awareness of God would become dehydrated and die. And as the Southern Baptist minister cried: 'Lord,' he said (this really isn't my style!), 'Lord, we can't hold much, but we can overflow lots.'

And so, whether we clap hands in our worship and cry aloud, or tread reverently the well-worn paths of our liturgy, we should demonstrate a joy which is as contagious as it is genuine, and our love and joy should overflow lots so that others are irrigated by it.

3 *Sunday morning and Monday morning*

Within the life of God the Holy Trinity, the Holy Spirit is the love between the Father and the Son, and this is why it is one work of the Holy Spirit in the Church and in the world to bring all men to that perfection of worship which is our destiny and the reason of our being.

That legend of the Tower of Babel which we had for our first reading this morning is at one level a piece of folklore seeking to explain the divisions between men, and their different languages. And then in the account of Pentecost we see men of all countries beginning to be united in the common language of worship. It is obvious that St Luke, who wrote the Acts of the Apostles, saw this as the reversal of Babel, the beginning of healing between nations. And this is a theme which reaches its full development in the Book of Revelation, in the vision of heaven:

> *After that I saw a huge number, impossible to count, of people of every nation, race, tribe and language. They were standing in front of the throne . . . and they shouted aloud, 'Victory to our God, who sits on the throne, and to the Lamb!'*

Now all this is heady stuff. I think it is right that when we are together on a Sunday, caught out of ourselves by the awareness of God, and thanking God for each other—it is right that we should remind ourselves of the great movements of God in history, and the culmination of all creation in the perfection of worship and praise. We are exhilarated by the ocean of God's love, its immensity and power. It is all good Sunday morning stuff.

But Christians also have to get up on Monday mornings. And that is when we need the awareness of God's presence in the ordinariness of things, in the routine and in the plodding duty.

Do you not realize that the very desire for God is placed within you by God the Holy Spirit? that the very dissatisfaction with oneself is a stirring by the Holy Spirit? that growth in the knowledge of God, the gradual integration of one's character, the facility of coping with life, these are the work of the Holy Spirit?

God is immensely more great than our little minds can imagine, yet our life is intimately bound up with his, and he is at work in the intimacies of our existence, in the decisions we make and the thoughts we think.

> Breathe on me, breath of God,
> Fill me with life anew,
> That I may love what thou dost love,
> And do what thou wouldst do.

God is closer than our breath, and he fill the whole world.

96

TRINITY SUNDAY

Our share in the heritage

Ephesians 1.3–14 (NEB)

1 *Every spiritual blessing*

'My religion is such a comfort to me.' This is one of those remarks which makes me shy like a startled horse, as I wonder which direction this shaft of wisdom is coming from.

Is it coming from some beleaguered soul who has found, in the midst of tension and distress, a sure ground for faith and hope, an assurance that in spite of everything he knows that in God's hand all is well, and all shall be well, and simply chooses those hackneyed words to express a deep and genuine conviction? In which case, as a fellow Christian, I accept what is meant and rejoice with him.

Or are those words, 'My religion is such a comfort to me,' the voice of complacency, the murmur of a soul asleep? And ought I not then, as a fellow Christian, to stir and prod this soul awake, lest he sleep for ever?

It has been my experience that immediately you begin in any way to respond to the love of God, against incredible inertia and reluctance as often as not, 'comfort', in the accepted sense of the word, is about the last thing you are going to receive. Because, far from sinking into static rest on the bosom of Mother Church (as our enemies imagine), you find yourself in a dynamic relationship with God, and others, which gives you no rest at all. An illustration of 'comfort', in the sense in which we call the Holy Spirit 'Comforter', is given in the Bayeux Tapestry. There a bishop, armed and mounted (bishops were bishops in those days!) is prodding his troops into battle with drawn sword. The inscription says, 'Bishop Odo *comforts* his troops'.

2 *Determined beforehand in Christ*

So if we are to use such a word, let us rescue it from the

97

image of a dummy which God pushes into our mouth to keep us quiet, for when we come to serve God we do not close our minds but open them. And we can begin to see the reason for the vehemence of that prohibition which thunders through the Old Testament: 'Thou shalt not make to thyself any graven image'—not because there is any danger of actually worshipping wood and stone (our heathen in his blindness was never as blind as that, and was far more subtle and spiritual than we imagine), but because an image is a limiting thing. You can encompass an image, and your heart and mind will cease to stretch. The literalness of that prohibition lost its point when Christ appeared, as the perfect image of the Father. Nevertheless St John, who of all writers in the New Testament works out this idea most thoroughly, can still warn, 'Children, keep yourself from idols'. Because far more dangerous than the image which you can dust and polish is the mental image you are hardly aware of, the formula which springs so readily to the lips, idols which must be dashed from the heart and mind if we are to remain free to be moved by the Holy Spirit, and to recognize the life of the Spirit in others. It is one work of the Holy Spirit to disturb a man or an institution that is becoming settled or somnolent, to break up what was taken as a settled outlook on life, in order that he may build up something better.

3 *To his praise and glory*

This would be clearer to us if our language made a clearer distinction between singular and plural pronouns. In practically all the reference to the work of the Holy Spirit, for example 'you are a temple of the Holy Spirit', the 'you' is not singular, as in our individualistic way we would imagine, but plural. We are not a lot of little temples, but growing together into one. The gifts of the Holy Spirit are given in community, the fruits of the Holy Spirit grow in community, the power of the Holy Spirit is evident in community.

It is together that we grow, it is in relationship that Christ is present, it is the Holy Spirit who binds all in one. And it is no accident that this language we use of Christ and his Church is the language we use of God himself, who is not a point of isolated Being, but is the perfection of relationship within the Holy Trinity.

It is to the Father that we pray and direct our worship, through Jesus Christ, of whose Body we are members, in the uniting power of the Holy Spirit—the grace of our Lord Jesus Christ, and the love of the Father, and the fellowship of the Holy Spirit.

> *And you too (plural again) . . . became incorporate in Christ and received the seal of the promised Holy Spirit; and that Spirit is in the pledge that we shall enter upon our heritage, when God has redeemed what is his own, to his praise and glory.*

PENTECOST 2

Come and let yourselves be built

1 Peter 2.1–10 (NEB)

1 *To offer spiritual sacrifices*

There is no such thing as a mass-produced choirboy, though in a few minutes you might be forgiven for thinking so, as we admit these boys to the choir. We welcome them to the Family of the Church here, and welcome their families too. They will tell their grandchildren that they were forced to come to church twice on Sundays, but you know as well as I do that nothing will keep them away. It is a funny old mixture of loyalty and friendship and clubbableness—and that dawning awareness of another dimension to life, which we describe by talking about God, and holiness, and love, and praise.

The tools of their trade are words and music, but it isn't all up here in the mind; there runs through it that other language of converse with God, which after all is the destiny of us all to employ throughout eternity.

Let us see in a boy's voice a lesson for us all in our use of God's gifts. First of all, it *is* a gift, and like the voices of us all can be used and misused for many things, for profanity as well as praise. And like all gifts it is a raw thing. If it is to be used in the service of God it needs to be offered back to him, and in community with others to be trained and developed.

> *Come and let yourselves be built, as living stones, into a spiritual temple.*

For this is how it is with all the things God gives us, not only voices. All his gifts come to us roughly shaped, and realize their potential only when offered back to him, in the community of those who love God. It was said of one man that, 'He had a lot to offer,' and I shall always remember the comment of another: 'But does he offer it?'—does he cling to it as his own possession, or does he offer it back to God? Only then can it become what it should be. 'O running stream of sparkling joy, to be a soaring human boy.' What we offer God is given back by him, transformed, pulsing with his life, touched with his glory.

2 *You have tasted that the Lord is good*

This is the principle which lies behind this service, this Eucharist. We offer what we have to God. We act it out in the procession of bread and wine and money, representative things. It is offered to God in union with the sacrifice of Jesus, and the life of God is offered back to us in Communion.

Have you considered how gently God deals with us?

> *Like the new-born infants you are, you must crave for*

100

pure milk (spiritual milk, I mean) so that you may thrive upon it to your soul's health.

In a moment I shall ask these boys two questions; 'Do you wish to become members of this choir?' (foolish question! foolish vicar!—how could you possibly keep them out?); 'Do you promise obedience to its rules and officers?' (dull question!, dull vicar!). Why don't I ask, 'Do you love God? Do you promise eternal devotion?' Because this is not how God deals with us. It is the next step he asks of us, not the next-but-one, let alone the next-but-ten. It is the attainable object he holds out to us, the reachable goal. So long as we are facing in the right direction: 'Do you turn to Christ?'

3 *A people claimed by God for his own*

Those of you who have been Christians for a long time—what if at the beginning of your pilgrimage you had had to bear the stresses and strains which now you take in your stride? Would you have ever taken the next step? And how, in those first stumbling steps towards God, would have coped with the depth of joy and assurance which now you enjoy? In a multitude of ways God has fed us with milk. He has led us step by step to deeper knowledge, deeper service, deeper love.

We do not stride through life like conquering heroes. I know some people give that impression, but it isn't true, you know. We stumble from step to step, from decision to decision, from milk to solid food. These boys will 'proclaim the triumphs of him who has called us out of darkness into his marvellous light.' It is in God's good time that that light will penetrate their souls. Their next step is pretty obvious. What is yours? What is the next thing you need to do? For you haven't yet arrived.

Eye has not seen, nor ear heard, nor the heart of man conceived, what God has prepared for those who love him.

PENTECOST 3

The new path of life

Romans 6.3–11 (NEB)

1 *When we were baptized*

When parents first look on their new-born child they are moved to wonder, as they come face to face with the mystery of life, and, if they don't ponder about life and where it comes from and how we are responsible for it, they must be cold fish indeed.

The sense of wonder is a religious reaction. And there is a very natural instinct common to all humanity, that the new life—so obviously a 'person' and not a 'thing'—should have his own name and a recognizable identity; that he should be recognized by the whole clan; and that a successful birth should be celebrated. And there is no difference at this level between the tribal whoopee in the jungle clearing, and Uncle Jack proposing the baby's health in a semi-detached in Penzance, as the assembled sisters and cousins and aunts ravage the christening cake. There is no difference in principle, because all are responding as human beings to the mystery of life. It is just that there is in this country, with one possible exception I shall mention, no suitable alternative to the Christian rite of initiation we know as Baptism.

Let us leave the sisters and cousins and aunts with their cake for a moment and consider another picture. There is no Confirmation service I have known for many years, when it has not been necessary first to baptize some of the candidates, because for some reason or other it never happened to them as infants. And this Baptism may immediately precede the Confirmation, or if we adopt the plan of the Alternative Service Book, be part of the same ceremony. So that Baptism plus Confirmation plus First Communion are seen as parts of one ceremony of Christian Initiation. This is not only the primitive pattern, but unless we do hold these three parts together, mentally if not physically, we cannot understand Christian Initiation.

Becoming a Christian is a highly personal experience, but it is not a private undertaking. Apart from a believing and worshipping community it has no meaning. In the combined rite of Initiation the great saving acts of God in Christ—his death and resurrection, his gift of the Spirit, his presence in the Eucharist—are re-enacted in the individual, within the Christian community. As Christ died, so do we die to our old nature in Baptism; as Christ was raised to new life, so are we born again; we are sealed and strengthened by the Holy Spirit; and are one with our Lord in Holy Communion. What is eternally true in God's work in Christ is earthed in the experience of each one of us. Baptism, Confirmation, membership of the Body, are all parts of one thing, and one cannot be understood without the others.

2 *Dead to sin*

We left the family with the christening cake. The pastoral need is for us to bring together these two pictures. We might begin to get somewhere if there were a moratorium on infant baptism for ten years, and we offered everyone the service of thanksgiving, which carries no promises, no commitment; but until that day we shall still have requests for infant Baptism.

It is a good thing if the parents can meet not just the vicar, but other members of the local Church. This immediately places the whole matter in the context of the worshipping community. 'Yes,' we say, 'we are happy to baptize your child, if that is what you really want, but let us explain Baptism, and what it entails. And first, *is* it what *you* want? Or is it what the child's grandmother wants? She belongs to a generation when you were decidedly odd if you didn't have children baptized. But you belong to a generation in which you are odd if you do. Grandmother comes every Saturday, and says, "Haven't you had him done yet?" until in desperation you come to

103

see the vicar. And do you want it for the right reasons? The wrong reasons are the old wives' tales that the child will not thrive until he has been not only inoculated and wormed, but christened as well. Or if he dies he will go straight to hell. Or your daughter will not be able to be married in church!'

So one goes on, and with parents who can reason you either part happily or bring them to Confirmation themselves. But you know that behind the inarticulate, beneath the superstition, there is a very deep desire to leave nothing undone that may benefit their child. They are stirring to a religious impulse. Love is one of God's gifts, and this is the growing point.

3 Alive to God

If this *is* to be a growing point the Christian community must in some way be involved. Christian couples must be prepared to visit and talk about Baptism, Baptisms ought to take place during the normal worship of the Church and the congregation prepared to be inconvenienced, and show by their attitude and welcome and care that Baptism is very important to us.

We recognize in the Gospel both a welcome and a challenge. If parents recognize in us a welcoming community which values its own Baptism so highly, this in itself is a challenge to look beyond the cake to some deeper understanding of what they mean when they are required to say, on behalf of their child, 'I turn to Christ'.

PENTECOST 4

All for his sons

>*Galatians 3.23–4.7 (TEV)*

1 *Father, my Father*

On Midsummer Eve beacon bonfires will be burning the length of Cornwall, starting in the west, each a signal for the next to be lit. No longer a signal that the Spaniards are coming (to steal our fish, as once they stole our wives), you must ask the Bards what they do signify. But it is a joyful and dramatic thing to do: hilltop catching fire from hilltop; instant recognition, urgent response; 'Go quickly and tell! Go quickly and tell.' So in today's Epistle St Paul speaks of the contagious fire of the Holy Spirit:

>*To show that you are his sons, God sent the Spirit of his Son into our hearts, the Spirit who cried out 'Father, my Father'.*

Or as the older translation said, 'Abba, Father', that affectionate form of address which Jesus used. The Holy Spirit lights a chain of souls throughout the world who catch fire from the divine love.

You will have known times when, like beacon responding to beacon, you have recognized in another person the light of Christ shining. And others will have seen it in you. You will have been another link in the vast network of God's Light:

>*You are the light of the world. A city built on a hilltop cannot be hidden. . . . Your light must shine in the sight of men, so that, seeing your good works, they may give praise to your Father in heaven.*

2 *Sons of the Father*

St Paul goes on to say,

105

Since you are his son, God will give you all that he has for his sons.

And lest those of you who are not male feel left out, he has already said that in baptismal status there is no difference:

> *between Jews and Gentiles, between slaves and free men, between men and women. You are all one in union with Christ Jesus.*

Our Lord's great parable of sonship is of course that of the prodigal son, the son who demands what his father freely gives, the son who is the light of his father's eye, and who goes on to hide that light in degradation and despair, so that the light becomes darkness. But even in the darkness there is the memory of that light, and like all living things he turns towards it. The prodigal son returns home; and like the watcher on the beacon hilltop eager for the first glimmer of light, the father makes his home ablaze with the warmth of welcome. Heart speaks to heart,

> *And the Spirit cries out 'Father, my Father'.*

3 *The other son*

But there is another son, the older brother, to whose jealous heart the light brings pain, and the warmth of his brother's welcome burns the bitterness deeper into his soul. Light not only signals joy, it brings to light the hidden things of the heart. And who has not felt sympathy for him?

We usually identify with the prodigal son, for we see in his forgiveness and restoration the overflowing love of God to us. But in the stories Jesus told there is never anything superfluous. Many of us within God's family must, if we are honest, identify ourselves with the older son: when we have been about God's work for a long

106

time, and the freshness has worn off; when we are sensitive about status and position; when God seems to have withdrawn from us that fresh awareness of him which marks our first steps in the Christian life (though of course he has withdrawn it only so that we may grow, as a father withdraws the supporting hand so that his son may walk); when discipleship has become routine and we are over-familiar with holy things. Then we are the older brother, a little tired, a little resentful, a little self-pitying.

But it is to the older brother that there is addressed the most wonderful statement in the whole of the New Testament:

> *'My son, you are always with me, and all that I have is yours.'*

On Midsummer Eve Cornwall will blaze again, from end to end, with the old beacon alarm of invasion. Come, Holy Spirit, invade our hearts with the fire of your love, that men may give praise to our Father in heaven, and urgently spread the light. Go quickly and tell of his love. Go quickly and tell.

PENTECOST 5

No coarse or flippant talk

Ephesians 5.1–10 (NEB)

1 *Christ knows*

The early summer sunshine always brings a procession of perambulators to the vicarage door. Babies who have hibernated are brought out into the open with a lust for water and instant Baptism. Among them once was a young mum, also wanting Baptism for her child, but at the parish next door. 'Would I give my consent?' It is a normal request, and not really a shopping round for the best terms. 'I suppose you were married there?' I asked. 'Oh yes, christened there and married there and Christ knows what.'

I bit back the reply, 'I am sure he does,' and proceeded with the matter in hand—which was also concerned with Christ, but a Christ whose name does not trip off our tongues quite so lightly, but is used by us with reverence and love.

Had I sold the pass again?

How do you react when holy things are bandied about in conversation? For I am sure you have to face it more often than I do. 'Damn!' 'Sorry Padre.' We walk on the knife edge between prudery and cowardice.

In the case of this dear affable mother it wasn't blasphemy. To blaspheme, to take the name of God in vain, you have to have some belief in God. Therefore only Christians can swear properly, which is why they don't. 'Have mercy upon us miserable sinners,' we sing. And we have a certain sympathy with the man who protested, 'I'm not a miserable sinner, I'm a cheerful one.' But 'miserable' here has its proper meaning of 'pitiable', and the man is to be pitied who has lost his scale of values, who has become disorientated, who has lost the sense of the holy.

2 These things are out of place

The episode with the pram on the way to the church next door tied in with a debate in the General Synod of the Church of England, which passed a motion deploring 'the extension and exploitation of blasphemy on radio and television'. Many of you may think that such protests do more harm than good. But if you never say anything, do you not condone?

We should be able to say to anyone, with complete respect, 'There are some things which are holy to me, and I will not have them dirtied or trivialized.' This can be at the level of the instinct which would make us all remove our shoes at a Buddhist shrine—out of respect for what others hold holy, without in any way compromising our belief in the uniqueness of Christ. And it can be at the level, which is surely ours as Christians, that 'Christ' to us is not just a title, that 'Jesus' is not just a name, but he is our brother and our friend, our saviour and our Lord, and we bow our head as we speak it. His holy Mother is our mother too, and the sacraments are expressions of his love and majesty and power. It is a matter of reverence— for words (which are sacred things), for people (who are loved by God), and for that which is holy. The man who has no reverence, no stopping point, ends up by having nothing. To us the words, 'Christ knows,' are literally true. The simple rule for Christians is that we take these things very seriously indeed, but don't take ourselves too seriously at all.

3 *At home in daylight*

Our easy acquiescent ways contrast with the suffering of our fellow Christians in rougher parts of the world. We need to see the death of the Archbishop of Uganda against the background of his own country. We learn that the blood of the martyrs is indeed the seed of the Church. The Church which produced that great and lovable archbishop, a man with Christ not only on his lips but also in his heart, grew from the seed of the first Uganda martyrs several generations ago. These were the boys who defied their tribal chief to learn about Jesus, and on being caught and refusing to deny the Lord they loved, were dismembered and burnt. It is said that before the smoke and flames did their work, there came clearly to the ears of those around the hymn, on the tortured lips of the children, 'Alleluia, sing to Jesus'—proclaiming Jesus to the world, because he was already in their hearts.

May Jesus be in our hearts, and on our lips—always with love, and never without reverence and awe.

PENTECOST 6

Forgiving each other

> *Colossians 3.12–17 (RSV)*

1 *Put on compassion*

Fierce and proud nations ensure that the countries of the Middle East have very little peace at all. Those of us who have been to those parts of the world have imprinted on our minds the bullet holes in the airport lounge, the wrecked and deserted towns, the helplessness of village communities with nowhere to shelter. Retribution, bullet for bullet, shell for shell: it is rough justice; eye for eye, tooth for tooth.

These nations inherit the mental climate in which St Peter asked Jesus about forgiveness: 'How often shall I forgive my brother?' And you know as well as I do, without going to the Middle East at all, the ferocity with which people pull each other to shreds; the family quarrels, the marriages which have dissolved into continuous recrimination. And you know, as well as I do, how difficult it is to forgive, and how terrifying the words of Jesus are: 'That is how my heavenly Father will deal with you unless you each forgive your brother from your heart.'

So glibly do the words of the Lord's Prayer pass our lips that we don't realize what we are saying: 'Forgive us our sins *as* we forgive those who sin against us': 'forgive me, just as much as I forgive old so and so'.

It isn't that God in a fit of irritation imposes conditions on our forgiveness, but that while there is spite and resentment in our hearts we render ourselves unforgivable.

'Oh,' people say, 'I can forgive anything done against me, but I can't forgive people who are cruel to children or who beat up old ladies.' Their sentiments become them, but forgiveness in such matters is not their business but for God—and the children and old ladies. There is in all of us the capacity for 'compounding for sins we are inclined to by damning those we have no mind to'.

Too often forgiveness is disregarded because it is confused with condoning, with pretending that things are not what they are, that evil does not matter. Whereas, for our forgiveness Christ suffered death on the Cross. That is what it costs God to forgive, and any forgiveness we may offer, when all our senses are screaming out for revenge, for not letting them get away with it—any forgiveness we offer must have a hint of the same cost.

2 *An eye for an eye*

But doesn't it say in the Bible, 'an eye for an eye and a tooth for a tooth'? Oh yes, it does. But the Bible is not a great monolith. It is a story of gradual revelation, of growing awareness of the nature of God, so that you are going to have a lot of bloody revenge in it before you come to the grace of the Gospel. And when that law was proclaimed—an eye for an eye and a tooth for a tooth—it was a merciful law. It was enshrined to limit revenge, to end the kind of blood-feud which was insatiable. It was a time when, if I knocked out your eye, you knocked out both of mine; and one of my teeth gone meant you lost all yours, upper and lower dentures. 'No!' said the prophets, those who were a step ahead in understanding the nature of God, 'you shall not exceed just recompense, because until that lesson is learnt you can't go on to learn the next one: "What does the law require of you, but to do justly, to love mercy, and to walk humbly with your God."' Dear Bible-quoter, don't forage in the Old Testament to justify your revenge, but look to that green hill outside Jerusalem, where the Son of God asked forgiveness for those who nailed him to the Cross. Look to the cost to God of your own forgiveness.

Let us look for a clue to the way we should behave in how Jesus identified himself with sinful human nature, and see how we are required to identify ourselves with all other men and women. It is often said that on a higher

111

level than condemnation is our ability to say, 'There, but for the grace of God, go I'. It is a precarious sort of attitude, but it does at least bring God into the situation. But it remains an argument from our own strength, and who are we to sit in judgment? There is a far higher degree of identification, and of honesty, if instead of saying, 'There, but for the grace of God, go I,' when faced with some enormity of human conduct, we can say, 'There go I!'.

For over-riding all our sense of outrage, and the wounds we receive from others, is our own desperate need of forgiveness. The lady next door is intolerably spiteful, but her spite pales into insignificance beside the continuous injury I do to God by my lukewarmness and lack of love. The wounds we receive from others are just not in the same class as the wounds in the hands of Christ.

3 *Giving thanks to the father*

Let us try to understand forgiveness—the forgiveness we offer to others—not so much as calculating how we shall react, as an attitude, an attitude to life and to all others we meet in that life. So that we do not sit down and calculate the terms on which we can say, 'I forgive you!' If we do we might get what we deserve. But if we are conscious all the time of what we owe to God—our life and existence and the hope of glory and our own forgiveness, then we shall go to others as forgiven sinners ourselves, and forbearance and true tolerance will grow in us. Because we shall be learning to see ourselves with God's eyes we shall begin to see others with those eyes too.

The way out of resentment is to look for something good in the other person, and to thank God as the source of that good. In that way we shall lift ourselves from confrontation to awareness of God.

> *Whatever you do, in word or deed, do everything in the name of the Lord Jesus, giving thanks to God the Father through him.*

PENTECOST 7

Love keeps no score of wrongs

1 Corinthians 12.27–13 end (NEB)

1 *Quick to take offence*

Last Tuesday evening I murdered twenty-three Cub Scouts. Not really, of course. It was only a game, and I murdered them only by surreptitious winks. So if my eye twitches this morning and all the Cubs fall down, don't be surprised.

I don't know that I am much of a psychologist, but I suppose there is something in the theory that playing at murder, and saying, 'Bang! you're dead!,' helps us to get a lot of aggression out of our system in a harmless way—like a sort of lightning conductor dispersing what could be a destructive and devastating force.

But if I'm not much of a psychologist I am sufficiently introspective, looking in on myself, to recognize the springs of aggression in myself, and to recognize when it is directed against me. Priests tend to attract a fair amount of aggression, though usually it is well disguised. It's part of the job, I suppose. You can't hit God, so you take it out on the chap with his collar the wrong way round.

There is a kind of religious aggression. What about St Paul? All that zeal against the Christians. Was it all zeal, or was there some 'aggro' too? 'Always mistrust the man who claims only the highest motives'—that can be a cynical recommendation, or it can be a realistic awareness that the motives of all of us are mixed.

When Saul became Paul, when he became a Christian, he didn't become a different kind of person. He was still zealous, still forceful. But the zeal and the force became positive—they were no longer directed *against* people, but were used *for* God. It was as if his personality had found its true direction.

113

2 *Gloating over other men's sins*

How's your aggro? When you are on your own, what are you thinking about other people? Are you inventing devastating conversations which always leave an opening for your crushing reply? (unlike real conversations of course, where you think of the really juicy bits afterwards!). Do you mull over and over again the old injuries. Do you harbour resentment?

No, you're not odd. Don't be afraid. You are not odd, but you have lost your sense of direction. 'Come with me,' said Jesus. And why did they? He didn't harangue them, or twist their arms; he didn't exercise a kind of aggression hidden under good motives.

They followed Jesus because he was supremely attractive—as holiness, closeness to God, always is. Saul followed Jesus and became Paul, and all the fierce longings of his heart were drawn one way, attracted by Christ. He wrote the Hymn of Love, which is our Epistle today. Pay attention to all the things he says love is not—boastful, conceited, rude, quick to take offence—and you will have a glimpse of the man who was Saul, and you will see why Paul explores the nature of love with the delight of discovery. It was part of his discovery of Christ, for Christ's are the only motives which are single and pure. He is not working out his frustrations on you. You can't really be bullied into loving God, or be frightened into serving God, or be argued into knowing God. You can, in the end, only be attracted *by* God.

3 *Love will last for ever*

We are just about in the middle of our preparation for the next Confirmation and we keep coming back to this point—that when all the instruction and discussion is done, there is the simple question asked by the Bishop 'Do you turn to Christ?'. And you don't have to pass any exams, and you don't have to be clever. You don't even have to be particularly good (God will look after that). But you do have to be able to say, 'I turn to Christ'. 'All

114

you have to do,' says Jesus, 'is to *want* to love me.'

Countless generations of men and women and boys and girls have found themselves able to say, 'I turn to Christ,' and this has been the beginning of the discovery of love, the gift of peace, and seeing themselves and others as Christ sees them.

Not 'Bang, you're dead!,' but 'Alleluia, you're beginning to come alive!'

PENTECOST 8

Self-indulgence

Galatians 5.16–25 (JB)

1 *Factions and envy*

It is evident to the least observant eye that our ancestors were of a hardier breed. It did not occur to them to provide toilets in churches, and with our sturdy independence there are many churches with none today. Ours is an incontinent age which demands a comfort station for every hundred pews. Nor were they too good at heating their churches. No doubt in the eighteenth century box pews, at least those belonging to the gentry, were furnished with little stoves (for the incontinence of that age was in the length of their sermons), but *any* warmth was a luxury. Now we come from centrally heated homes and actually expect to take our coats off in church. Our churchwardens, indeed, are not allowed to wear them, lest it puts ideas of coolness into people's heads.

The point I labour to make is by no means original: it is that the luxuries of one generation become the necessities of the next. And for the Christian, aware of the debilitating effect of luxury, and aware of his suffering brothers and sisters throughout the world, this poses a moral problem. What is proper to a Christian lifestyle in

115

the 1980s? Very few can solve the problem by opting out from the culture in which they live, and it would be artificial to reduce the quality of life to a dull grind, especially it if deprived one's family of the capacity to enjoy, or wilted the flowering of the human spirit.

2 *Luxury*

To avoid all kinds of horrible heresies, it is essential to maintain that things in themselves are not evil. If they are not necessarily good, they are morally neutral. It is our attitude to them and our use of them that is questioned. And they are of three kinds. There are some which are necessary, which God always provides, and these are far fewer than most of us imagine—the things we call the bare necessities of life. Then there are those things which are useful, which add to our comfort and well-being, which set us free from scratching for an existence, to sing and dream and enjoy. The third kind are luxuries.

As a way of pandering to ourselves we have tended to emasculate the word 'luxury'. It originally meant debauchery, extravagance. In medieval Latin it is the word from which we derive 'lust'. It was more like that catalogue of failings with which St Paul berates the Galatians. The word 'luxury' hardly has a respectable ancestry. At the very least 'luxuries' are things in excess of our legitimate needs. We live in a society battered by attempts to sell us luxuries. You note that it is never hammers and spades which are advertised on television.

3 *Poor in spirit*

It would however be a false pharisaic trail which led us to compose lists of what is acceptable or not, because circumstances alter cases, and our Lord is far more concerned with attitudes of heart and mind: if our heart is set on God we shall enjoy the good things of life, but not be dependent on them. And this, you know, is what lies behind that rather strange beatitude, 'Blessed are the poor in spirit'. This certainly does not mean those we

116

would call poor-spirited. The poor in spirit are those who in attitude are not possessive or acquisitive, who can accept pleasures or do without them with no disturbance of the main direction of their life. They are those who do not take life for granted, but accept it with gratitude; those who accept life as a gift, and nothing they think they have a right to. In their spirits they are poor and are possessive about nothing. This, of course, cuts right across all divisions of actual wealth, because we are concerned with attitude, and whether you are poor or rich you can be covetous.

> *You cannot belong to Christ Jesus unless you crucify all self-indulgent passions and desires.*

When Job had lost all his possessions, lost his family, lost his friends,

> *he fell to the ground. He worshipped and said, 'Naked I came from my mother's womb, naked I shall return. The Lord gave, and the Lord has taken back. Blessed be the name of the Lord.'*
> *In all this Job committed no sin, nor offered any insult to God.*

PENTECOST 9

The sword of the Spirit

Ephesians 6.10–20 (RSV)

1 *Alert with all perseverance*

I wonder if you can guess what natural human function this describes: 'An abrupt strong expiration, followed by a series of expiratory–inspiratory microcycles superimposed upon the larger expiratory movements. The mouth is opened, the teeth are bared, and there is a generalized tremor, sometimes amounting to a convulsion.'

Before you send for a strait-jacket, let me tell you that that all describes a LAUGH, and before you resolve never to laugh again, let us just say that the definition demonstrates how remote from instinct you can get, when you move from experience to the clinical description of experience.

It is with this awful warning in mind that I venture to speak about the Holy Spirit; for we must acknowledge first that if there were no Holy Spirit, and if he were not at work in us, we should not be here in church at all.

Let me come back to this point via another illustration. If we look back over our lives we might well say that in that time only a very few 'spiritual experiences' stand out—a memorable communion here, a turning-point confession there, a converting confrontation somewhere else. These are like the mountain peaks in what might be miles and years of country very dull indeed. When this is pointed out to me, as it sometimes is in criticism of acre after acre of mediocre sermons, I say, 'Well, compare sermons to the meals you have eaten over the same period. Only a few stand out as memorable, either from what you had to eat, or where you ate it, or the company you ate it in. But—and this is the point—unless you had been nourished over that period by good and wholesome fare, even if none of it stands out as memorable, you would have faded away from malnutrition.'

2 *Put on the whole armour*

So with the Holy Spirit. Before we start getting excited about his greater manifestations, let us first acknowledge his ordinary work, his unspectacular achievement, his normal nourishment of the Christian life, without which we would not be here at all, without which we would have faded away through malnutrition, without which our love of God and service of Christ would be extinct.

I say this because in our generation many Christians are

118

rediscovering a further depth to life in the Holy Spirit, a new (because really old) exhilaration in the love and service of God, in a movement which is described as 'charismatic' or 'pentecostalist'. As always with enthusiasts, there is a temptation to say, 'Unless you have had this particular experience your discipleship is not genuine.' It is undoubtedly true that there is a greater openness and joy in the whole Church, rubbed off from this enthusiasm. But the point I want to make is that without the Holy Spirit there can be no discipleship at all, and where there is undoubted discipleship, there undoubtedly is the Spirit at work.

Bearing in mind, from our definition of a laugh, how far into nonsense we can stray in the clinical description of experience, let us keep to what we see. When we see an old and faithful Christian showing more and more the fruits of the Spirit—love, joy, long-suffering, patience—here, we say, is the work of the Holy Spirit. When we are encouraged by the zeal and enthusiasm of the young Christian—here, we say, is the work of the Spirit. When we are challenged by the Christian prophet calling us to social justice, impatient with excuses and half-truths and compromise—here, we say is the Spirit at work. When we see a congregation growing in love and expectancy so that from this womb there come to birth many vocations—here, we say, is a community of the Holy Spirit. When in a district we see the Christian congregations growing together in love and understanding and unity—here is the Spirit of unity at work. When we discover among ourselves a burning desire for mission, a looking outwards into the community in which we live, here too we see a stirring of the Holy Spirit.

3 *As I ought to speak*

Just as we cannot see the air which stirs the trees but know it only by its effects, so it is with the Holy Spirit, whom we cannot see, but whose work we can recognize. If we want a definition, here it is: 'The Holy Ghost is of the Father

119

and of the Son, neither made, nor created, nor begotten, but proceeding . . . and in this Trinity none is afore, or after other, none is greater, or less than another, but the whole three Persons are co-eternal together, and co-equal.' But the Holy Spirit is our life, and we cannot reduce life to a definition. Let us remain within our own experience. Just think for a moment of the breath you are taking. Allow yourselves to become conscious of the act of breathing. . . . We are surrounded and permeated by the air, but until we stopped to think we were unaware of the force which sustains us. So let us stop to think of God the Holy Spirit, surrounding and permeating us. Let us grow in the habit of becoming aware of him, of the grace and love and power he brings us, and let us learn to say, 'Thank you, Holy Spirit!'

PENTECOST 10

Our common life in Christ

Philippians 2.1–11 (NEB)

1 *Anything to stir the heart*

Sherlock Holmes showed in *The Case of the Purloined Letter* that if you want to go unnoticed, it is easier to do so in a crowd than on your own. It is the same principle which can make large cities lonely places—or dangerous places, come to that. Because in a crowd no one cares.

That is how I nearly didn't save someone from drowning. It was many years ago, in my sporting days (which weren't very sporting, and certainly a long time ago!). I was in a crowded swimming pool, and for some time I watched a small boy jumping up and down in water which was just too deep for him, wondering why he seemed to prefer having his head under the water most of the time. Then I thought that perhaps he didn't, so I put out my hand. The way he grasped it showed he was rather glad of a rescue.

It is a sad fact that in an unheeding crowd people can perish within reach of a hundred helping hands, if the minds directing the hands are not alert. Another version of this tale is that of the old person in a block of flats, whose fate is revealed only by the mounting newspapers in the door or the milk bottles outside it. All this can be within reach of a hundred helping hands, if only the minds directing those hands had been alert.

And it is an unhappy fact that it is possible for members of a Christian congregation slowly to lose grip of their faith and drift and sink away. People do get out of their depth in doubts and worries, and slowly lose their consciousness of Christ—and all this within reach of a hundred helping hands if only we were more alert.

2 *Look to each other's interests*

We are, of course, all at different levels of competence in the swim of life. There are those of us glad of the chance to splash about at the shallow end. There are those who will always need water-wings. There are the spectacular high-divers. There are those with only one toe in. And there are some of you, and thank God for you, who prowl round the edge of this pool, with a loving and sensitive eye, and when you see someone getting into difficulties, you do something about it. Or if you can't do something about it yourself you alert the professional life-saver: 'Look, I wouldn't be surprised if a lifebelt wouldn't be of some help there!' Don't assume that the priest has some special kind of aerial which picks up waves of distress. He would rather be told twenty times than not at all. And if you are drowning shout for help! But don't say, 'No one from the Church has been,' when faithful laypeople have been exercising their ministry of care. What you mean is that the vicar hasn't been! The pathetic thing so often is how little help is needed: no need for the dramatic rescue, the leaping fully clothed in a blaze of publicity; just the helping hand, a little bit of alertness.

121

3 *Your bearing towards one another*

There are many visitors here this morning. It is one of the nice things about a seaside church in summer. I hope you feel you had a good welcome. One of the difficulties is that visitors tend to come to church early, while the locals slope in at the last minute. Of course, the person next to you may be a visitor too, and if you don't speak to each other you will both accuse us of being unfriendly! And if you think us a funny old lot, remember that that always has been said about the friends of Jesus. They used to complain about it then—that he kept company with such nasty people. So if the person next to you is nasty, don't be surprised! Later in the service, when we come to 'the peace' you will find that we are a little shy of actually shaking hands or kissing each other. It is not because we are afraid of catching anything, and our welcome is no less sincere.

'Let your bearing towards one another,' says St Paul, 'arise out of your life in Christ Jesus.'

When strangers meet, it is one of the ploys of social behaviour to try to discover something in common, or some acquaintance you both know. As we gather here we know that we have in Jesus someone whom we all know. 'If you are a friend of Jesus, you are a friend of mine.' It is his love which is our common assurance, and the assurance to each of us that we shall never sink without trace.

PENTECOST 11

The serving community

2 Corinthians 4.1–10 (NEB)

1 *Your servants for Jesus' sake*

Though you might not immediately suspect it from the selection of readings this morning (and it must be difficult to keep the selection fresh by the time you get to Pentecost 11), the theme for today is the Church as the serving community.

If we think back to the Last Supper we hear our dear Lord say, 'You call me Master and Lord, and rightly; so I am. If I, then, the Lord and Master have washed your feet, you should wash each other's feet. I have given you an example so that you may copy what I have done to you.'

So the Church, as Christ's Body, is here to serve. And you recall the words of Saint Teresa:

> Christ has no body on earth but yours,
> no hands but yours,
> no feet but yours.
> Yours are the eyes through which his compassion
> will look upon the world.
> Yours are the feet with which he will go about doing
> good.
> Yours are the hands with which he will bless men
> now.

2 *Pots of earthenware*

Now, what do you mean by a 'serving Church'? Go back some years and the question would never have been asked, for the answer was obvious. These words come from an account written by a child of a vicarage, of his experiences in the depression of the early 1930s. 'The parish was one which included both an area of poverty and an area of comparative prosperity. The two areas marched side by side; and it was precisely on the boundary that the church stood. Its geographical position symbolized at least a part of its activity and importance: for through the church, and stimulated by it, there passed a considerable traffic of concern and practical help from one area to the other.'

This instantly conjures up the picture, and for quite a few of you the memory, of the Sisters of this parish, and the network of parish visitors caring in a practical way for those who lived in the little courts of New Street and around the harbour. It would be unkind to criticize this as 'paternalistic'. We must never sneer at this ambulance work—the sheer quantity of it, done in the name of Christ, is deeply moving.

Nowadays, to cope with physical relief, we have the Welfare State. But the Welfare State has only worked, and it is becoming increasingly obvious that it will only work, with goodwill. And one important task today for those with Christian perception is to fill the gaps, to interpret the Welfare State, to make it work.

3 *Out of darkness let light shine*

But for an understanding of what Christian service involves we must look deeper.

A few years ago I went up to the headquarters in England of a small African mission. We had some money to hand over, and the meeting of the English Committee seemed a good opportunity to do so. We waited in the appointed room for some time, and then there came upon the ear, from down the corridor, little scratchings and twitterings, and there staggered into the room (and it took several minutes for the gathering to be complete) a number of very, very old ladies, with pince-nez, ear trumpets, crutches, surgical corsets and other life-support systems. The cruel impulse was to laugh. But these were heroines of the faith, who had given their lives as pioneers of the Church in Africa, who had fought ignorance and

124

disease and lions with equal courage, a total of hundreds of years of the Serving Church. One old lady asked how far I had had to come. 'About ten miles,' I said. 'Ah then,' she said, 'you will have walked.'

And I think of the old Missionary College of St Augustine in Canterbury. If you have ever been there you will recall how the walls of the chapel are covered with marble memorial plaques, memorials to the young men who in the last century had gone out to the Ivory Coast, knowing they were going to certain death from disease, for none lasted more than one or two years.

And this brings us deeper still into the mystery of service. Christ's hands and feet still serve the world in countless ways, and where this is true service it reveals the deeper mystery, that Christ's hands and feet bear the wounds and prints of nails. For suffering is never far from true service. For this reason: that the suffering, the passion of Christ, is the one thing in the long history of the world that has ever done any real good, in the sense that it begins to cure the source of man's disease and not merely the symptoms. The sacrifice of Christ begins to restore that harmony between God and man which has always been God's intention and desire.

And those who would offer this service, those who would be the feet of Christ in this world with which he will go about doing good (for he has no other) and those who would be his hands in the world with which to bless men now (for he has no other) will find that they are wounded, and will share in some way in the suffering of Christ. This is known on the most superficial level by anyone who lifts a hand in the public good. The great Eleanor Roosevelt once said, 'You learn to live with, but you never get used to, the calumny and spite you meet in public service.'

Let us then be prepared for the hands to be wounded and the feet crippled and the body torn. And yet to allow through our eyes only his compassion to look upon the world.

Wherever we go we carry death with us in our body,

*the death that Jesus died, that in this body also life
may reveal itself, the life that Jesus lives.*

PENTECOST 12

Our estimate of any man

2 Corinthians 5.14–6.12 (NEB)

1 *Worldly standards*

The trouble about mentioning names in church is that you
tend to embarrass people. So I apologize in advance to
those of you called Paul, and I will explain to your friends
and enemies that my remarks are not about you, but
about another Paul I know.

We had taken our church choir on a singing tour of
Germany, and I had gone along as well. Some of them
seemed to regard me as a kind of mascot to ensure good
weather, though I assured them that I was in the 'sales'
department of the Church, and not 'management'.

And sitting next to me on this coach winding up the
Rhine Valley was Paul. In fact he was almost sitting *on*
me. Because Paul was one of the heartier lads, about
sixteen at the time; and in the way that hearty people have
he had dominated the journey by his boisterous behaviour
and rather fruity conversation.

But at the moment I am talking about the conversation
had died away, and I was thinking my own thoughts, and
he was humming snatches from what the choir had been
singing: 'Tum tum te tum,' he hummed, 'tum, tum te tum,
Sweet Jesus say "Amen".'

Now this was so far from his usual style that at first I
thought he was being a bit cynical and that a word of
reproof was necessary. But I glanced sideways and saw
that he was lost in a kind of reverie, thinking his own
thoughts, lost in himself, as we say. So, instead of being
cross, I thought 'What a funny mixture people are!' and

126

'How do we balance the kind of people that we are with the sort of language which is placed on our lips when we come to church?'.

2 *A new order has already begun*

Here was Paul. The Paul we saw most of the time was rather noisy (sorry, all the Pauls here, who are of course nothing of the kind!). He was the life and soul of the party. He couldn't speak German, and the German girls couldn't speak English (isn't it strange how 'Abroad' is so full of foreigners?), yet they were round him like bees round a honey-pot. And yet here was this other side of him: the dreamer, the singer subordinating his own gifts to the group of the choir; one whose job in the choir was to voice holy thoughts about God.

It isn't just Paul I am talking about—I should think that is obvious. It was a girl of Paul's age who once said to me, 'I'm one person at school, another person with my friends, and another person in church. Which is the real me?' We are all quite mixed-up enough to know what she meant.

And on our lips, which we use at other times for blasphemy and hate and dirt, we put, when we come to worship, sublime words and thoughts about God, about our love for him, about his beauty and majesty—ideas far too great to express the way we actually feel, but which do express an ideal, in response to the very deep thoughts longing of our hearts.

In a few moments we shall be stretching out our hands to receive Jesus in Communion, and the chalice will be placed to our lips. Hands too, in which the host will be placed, can be used hatefully as well as helpfully. Which is the real us? Those in the choir are beautifully dressed and look pure and holy. Then when people see them going over to the pub and the boys jumping on the gravestones they say we are hypocrites. Nothing of the sort! You are a hypocrite only if you pretend to be something you are not. We know we are not holy, we know we are this strange

127

mixture of good and bad. We are just not sure which is the real us.

3 *This is the work of God*

The answer is that both parts are real. The trouble is that we are so aware of the grubby part that we think our good thoughts and our longing to serve God are a kind of dream. We are sometimes even ashamed that we have been moved by the holiness of God, or that we have been caught out of ourselves in worship. We laugh it off and say, if we admit it at all, 'Oh, I must have been carried away!'

Don't ever believe that. Both parts are real—the ordinariness and scruffiness of everyday life (like the Paul we saw most of the time) *and* the aspiration, the reaching out (like the Paul I overheard by accident), the deliberate placing of ourselves in the stream of adoration and worship.

You see, deep in the heart of everyone is a longing which can be satisfied by no one and by nothing except God. It is simply the way we have been made as human beings. St Augustine put it like this: 'You (meaning God) have made us for yourself, and our heart shall find no rest until it rest in you.'

The other thing I remember about Paul on that journey is the enormous plastic bag he brought to keep his surplice clean. And even this need for a clean surplice has its heavenly counterpart. Our heavenly Father looked on the human nature he had created, and finding it rather grubby, said to his Son, 'Go and wash it.' So Jesus, Son of Mary, and Son of God Most High, assumed our flesh, our hands and lips, and presented it spotless before the Father.

> *His purpose in dying for all was that men, while still in life, should cease to live for themselves, and should live for him who for their sake died and was raised to life. With us therefore worldly standards have ceased to count in our estimate of any man.*

You and I, and Paul, and everyone else God has created out of love, are in that glorified humanity. This is the real truth about us.

Sweet Jesus, say AMEN.

PENTECOST 13

They stopped their ears

Acts 7.54–8.1 (RSV)

1 *When they heard these things*

Some years ago there appeared an advertisement in the 'For Sale' columns offering a parrot for sale. 'Good speaker,' it said, 'but unsuitable for a vicarage.' There were many inquiries, quite a few from vicarages! But, fascinating though a talking parrot may be, it can speak only, as we say, 'parrot fashion'. Like a computer you get out only what you put in. It is a far cry from the free speech of free men expressing what is in their heart and soul.

Parents wait with eager impatience for their children to speak. The formation of the infant gullet, and the frequency of wind, mean that the first sounds usually come out as 'dada', much to the consolation of that gentleman.

Some parents, however, wait with ever growing anxiety for their children to speak. The chances are that if a child does not talk it is because he is deaf. He cannot imitate what he cannot hear.

That is the normal procedure in diagnosis—finding out why there is no intelligent sound.

2 *They stopped their ears*

There is a spiritual parallel. If we say, 'I find it difficult to pray,' or 'Worship has lost its attraction for me,' or 'I find it difficult to say the words in church with any degree of sincerity,' it is another way of saying that we are spiritually dumb.

So let us apply our first rule of diagnosis, and ask ourselves, 'Am I speechless because I have ceased to hear?' Then we apply the second rule of diagnosis: 'Have I ceased to hear because I have allowed all quietness to be squeezed out of my life? I am surrounded by noise and I am hounded by events. Have I stopped setting aside times in the day unalterably given over to God?' For if we do not listen we do not hear, and if we do not hear God, we cannot adequately praise him.

Or have I ceased to hear because I have *refused* to listen? We want to persist in some particular sin, so we refuse to listen to our conscience, until conscience itself is dumb. We want to persist in something the Church declares to be wrong, and, while closing our ears to the Church, complain that the Church herself will not listen. There are more ways than one of being deaf, and none more effective than refusing to listen. How significant that the persecutors of St Stephen 'cried out with a loud voice', drowning what they did not want to hear. 'They cried out with a loud voice and stopped their ears.'

So, many people pursue exotic consultations and remedies, when a little simple listening would cure them—as with Naaman in the Old Testament. You remember Naaman—he was indignant and went off saying, 'Here was I thinking he would be sure to come out to me, and stand there, and call on the name of the Lord his God. Surely I have got bigger and better rivers to bathe in than this muddy little Jordan.' And his servants, who do deserve full marks for courage, said to him, 'My father, if the prophet had asked you to do something difficult would you not have done it? All the more reason then when he says to you "bathe and be clean".' So he went down and immersed himself seven times in the River Jordan as Elisha had told him to do, and 'his flesh because clean once more, like the flesh of a little child.' In the same way people scorn the Christian equivalent of the little river—look at the sacraments! What can they do for me?

But those who in simple attention and obedience repent and believe the Gospel, find in these simple outward things the power of God himself, and the way to wholeness and holiness.

Too often we are like the woman who, it was always said, 'enjoyed bad health'. We don't want to be cured and we have closed our ears to the Gospel. And because we don't hear, our speech is defective, our worship is starved, and our witness to others is inaudible. It has always been true that those through the ages who have proclaimed the Gospel most convincingly have been those who first listened to God.

3 *I see the heavens opened*

One day a deaf and dumb man was brought to Jesus. He took him aside, in private, away from the noise of the crowd, put his fingers into his ears and touched his tongue. *Ephphatha!* Be opened! And his ears were opened and the ligament of his tongue was loosened, and he spoke clearly. Their admiration was unbounded. 'He has done all things well. He makes the deaf hear and the dumb speak.'

Lord Jesus, take me away often to that intimacy with you, and touch the ears of my soul that I may hear you, so that my tongue may be loosened and speak of your glory, and men may say that you have done all things well.

PENTECOST 14

The family

> *Ephesians 5.25–6.4 (JB)*

1 *Family life*

Every Christmas carol service we hear the same blood-thirsty lesson about Abraham lisped by innocent lips: 'Because you have done this, because you have not refused me your son, your only son, I will shower blessings upon you . . .'. Bully for Abraham. We know of course that in the end Abraham did not actually have to sacrifice his son. Bully for Isaac. But you notice that his right to do so is never questioned. So when we speak of families and fathers and obedience of children we have to realize that the family that lives next door with 2.3 children and a hamster has not always been typical. Fathers once had absolute power of life and death over their families, but family life is always changing. Now even the economic restraints which bound households together have been loosened, people live longer, and the skills of one generation are out of date before the children of the next have left school. And, in school, when you speak to an assembly of children, you have to realize that by the law of averages many of them will come from homes broken in some way. 'One-parent families' is the euphemism we use, though to an older generation that is a contradiction in terms. You have to be very sensitive to their feelings, and be careful how you use terms like 'family' and 'father'. For when we speak of God as Father the term has always needed interpretation. Are we calling up pictures of a patriarch like Abraham; or of the man seen by arrangement of the court once a week; or of the loving presence of a parent in the home?

Here is a quotation about families which I find strangely comforting (I will tell you why afterwards): 'The children of today love luxury. They have bad manners, contempt for authority, and disrespect for their elders.

They no longer rise when older people enter the room. They contradict their elders, wolf their food, and tyrannize their parents.' I find that comforting because it was said by Socrates, in 399 BC!

2 *The church family*

There has been a fashion to refer to the local church as a family, although—or perhaps because—there are few complete natural families in any congregation. Certainly we are quarrelsome and get on each other's nerves, as in any family. There are tensions between the generations, as in any family. But, on the positive side, the church is the womb in which we are brought to birth in the faith, and the sphere where we are nurtured in it. We assist each other in the growth in holiness, and we tread the picture galleries of the family homestead and see the family likeness in the portraits of the saints. But above all the church is like a family in its givenness: we do not choose our fellow members any more than we choose Aunty Mabel. The church is not a club of like-minded members, but a living organism whose parts are dependent on each other.

So, if we are asked who we are, we give our Christian name and our surname. The Christian name is our name within the Christian family of the Church, our surname roots us firmly in the currents of humanity which brought us to birth. It shows how little we can really be separated from our family: the traits of our character, the colour of our hair (though that is perhaps not a good example), and the very fact of our existence, are derived from others. I am always the child of my parents, whether they love me or not, whether or not I know them.

3 *Implications*

St Paul deliberately chooses the union of man and woman as an image of the Church: 'A man must leave his father and mother and be joined to his wife. . . . This mystery

133

has many implications, but I am saying that it applies to Christ and his Church.'

Fine words! But just for a moment let us be honest with ourselves. Think of your own marriage, and your own family. Is that an image of Christ and his Church? This human nature we carry about with us, which *is* us, this hungering lusting flesh, well, St Paul also compared the Church to this—a body with many parts.

What is he saying about us? What is this talk about bodies and families?

I think some of his 'many implications' are the following.

Although each one of us is a unique creation by God, we are not isolated creations. We are, first, part of the family of man, and therefore created for life in community. And the intimate community of family and friendship is in some ways a reflection of that perfect society which is the Holy Trinity himself.

Then, if we are to come to that perfection God has planned for us it will not be by discarding our human nature but by glorifying it: 'Grace perfects nature, it does not destroy it.' We are not angels, nor will we ever be angels, pure spirit. We are this odd experiment by God, a union of physical and spiritual, and it is no contradiction when we speak of human love with all its sweaty concomitants, and in the same breath speak of the love of God. The trial of Lady Chatterley was the wrong occasion to make that point, but there was a kind of mad logic in the attempt.

And thirdly, there is a deep mystery in our relationship with each other. Just as children will always be part of their parents, so all our relationships, mental or physical, are never casual, but have eternal consequences. I will for all time be the person who did this particular thing to that particular person.

But Christ has power to redeem all these, power to redeem our families, power to redeem our bodies, power to redeem our involvement with each other. 'Christ loved the Church,' says St Paul, 'and sacrificed himself for her,

134

to make her holy. He made her clean . . . so that when he took her to himself she would be glorious, with no speck or wrinkle or anything like that, but holy and faultless.'

PENTECOST 15

Those in authority

Romans 13.1–7 (JB)

1 *Civic occasions*

Every few weeks I do my duty as Chaplain to the Mayor. This means I have a special seat in the Council Chamber and open the meetings with prayer. I have no other voice in the deliberation though politely I stay as long as I can. There are some occasions when I can only pray and then run for it. The presence of a priest is a reminder that our rulers are answerable not only to the electorate, but to God; a reminder that every committee decision is in some way a theological decision—because it concerns man, who is made in the image of God. Whatever my presence may symbolize, I think it even better that three members of our congregation are on the council, and express their Christian commitment in that way.

Indeed it is not all that long since churchwardens *were* local government, before the civil and ecclesiastical functions divided. Jesus, and the society in which he lived, would have found any distinction between sacred and secular quite artificial, and the Jewish law was concerned just as much with the digging of drains as with the ceremonial of the temple. What we have to make sure, with civic services and similar occasions, is that the event is enhanced by the awareness of God.

2 *Authority and service*

Some years ago I was sent on a course for rural deans to

Windsor Castle. (That's a good bit of name-dropping if you like. When commenting on the increase in name-dropping a former Dean of Windsor is supposed to have replied, 'Yes, the Queen and I are getting rather worried by it!') But St George's House, Windsor is a conference centre, and the glory I enjoyed was purely reflected glory. So we shared the worship of St George's Chapel, and sat under the banners of the Knights of the Garter, and trod on the graves of kings, and touched things that royal hands had touched.

Such evidences of regal pomp excite different feelings in different people. Being rather simple and English I was moved by it all. But we heard of an overseas bishop who had said, 'It is as much as I can do to remain in this place—it is just this triumphalism which kept my people in subjection for generations. To find it in this chapel, in conjunction with the altar of Christ is almost more than I can stomach.'

I sympathize with his feelings and understand them, but I still think that there is a deeper mystery here than he perceived, in the conjunction of majesty with service. The older ones among us can look back, and recall how at a coronation the figure of the sovereign, tiny in the splendours of Westminster Abbey, grew as the symbols of human dignity were added one by one—mantle, sceptre, orb and crown; until as homage was paid that figure dominated the assembly. And then the symbols were stripped away again, and the sovereign left the throne to kneel in simplicity before the altar, to receive in Holy Communion the sovereign Lord of all.

This is the heart of the mystery of authority and service, and it remains true not only at that level, but also in the local Council Chamber when we discover that the provision of public toilets is equivalent to a three-penny rate. We are saying, 'In this strange business of the body politic (using the word politics in its clean meaning of the art of living together) we are not the final arbiters; we are answerable not only to a fickle electorate, but to God, who is not fickle at all, but consistent in his goodness and holiness and love.' The neck that bears the chain of office is bowed before a greater authority. A cat may look at a queen. It is man's greater dignity to look on God, and to be judged by that perfection.

3 *Establishment*

A little while ago a famous politician occupied the pulpit of St James' Piccadilly, and, searching round for a spanner to throw in the works, chose the rather rusty old one of disestablishment: 'Denationalize the Church of England!' The Church-State link in England has had some value in the past, and it has meant some recognition of Christianity by the State, and it has helped the Church to be comprehensive and to be involved pastorally with the whole community and not simply with gathered congregations. Indeed 'establishment' is not any one and single thing. It is a complex of laws and customs concerning the role and coronation of the sovereign, the role of bishops and methods of Church legislation, the privileges of the parish priest in his pastoral office, and many other things. 'Disestablishment' is itself a negative formula. It says what should be discarded. It would be better to ask, 'What is it desired that the Church should do, and be, different from what it does and is at present.'

Someone once asked that great man Michael Ramsey, when he was still Archbishop of Canterbury, 'What would you do to reform the Church of England?' The great man pondered. At last a response was seen to be working its way through to the great cliff-like face. The eyebrows twitched. 'I would begin,' he said, 'by reforming the Archbishop of Canterbury from the top to the bottom!'

By this I am sure he meant not only a reformation of his role, but a transformation of his person. And is this not where all reformation must begin? The Church in the parish is not the vicar conducting state prayers at council meetings. It is each one of us going about our daily lives and duties, where people will either meet Christ in us, or they will not.

137

Just as the Body of Christ exists in every portion of the host, so the whole Church is behind the individual countenance of every Christian.

PENTECOST 16

Let love be genuine

Romans 12.9–end (RSV)

1 *Never flag in zeal*

Each day we are faced with a hundred choices—whether to speak, or to keep silent, what to say, what to do. When we are rather new as Christians we feel we need a pocket reference book: how should I behave now? what should I say? We are very self-conscious indeed. To some extent we are playing a part. It happens when you become a vicar too—the new mantle does not fit very well.

What the new Christian hopes (and the new vicar for that matter) is that experience will bring with it what the old theologians called 'formation of character', so that our responses and our choices become not only right but instinctive.

But how if the responses and choices become so much a matter of instinct that while the outer shell, the façade, is preserved; behind it routine takes over, joy evaporates, we lose conscious touch with God, and we are distracted from that fellowship with Jesus which has been our motive and our inspiration? I doubt if there is any Christian (so be assured by this) who has not been distressed by this evaporation of the awareness of God, for a time, perhaps for a long time, particularly in the long haul of those middle years.

2 *Outdo one another in showing honour*

Can you imagine what it was like for Jesus once he

became well-known, and crowds gathered at the hint of his appearance? To be pushed and touched and pleaded with—imagine the smell of such a crowd on a hot day—and yet always that complete attention to the individual he was concerned with at the time, the concentration. And never, even at the greatest pressure, was there any faltering of his awareness of his heavenly Father. Nothing would distract him from that.

Well, it doesn't take much to distract us, does it? And do you find it gets worse when we come to church? There are two things I would like to say about this.

The first is local and domestic and rather obvious—that we can help each other over this matter of distraction. I find wholly good and natural the friendly greetings we give each other as we gather for worship, and the joyful exchange of shared experience at 'the peace', and as we leave. But there are moments when people should feel safe from intrusion. Monks and nuns are the first to admit that the community life of strong-minded people would soon crack without the 'Greater Silence'—hours when you do not attract the attention of others by word or act. So in this service, from the consecration to the dismissal, our minds should be on God alone. This kind of attention, of devotion, is our gift not only to God, but to each other.

3 *Constant in prayer*

The other point I want to make is that what really matters is not so much our success in avoiding distraction, at the motive and *intention* with which we go about things. It is, after all, the Christian duty of a Christian engine-driver to watch the signals, not to be dreaming about holy things. A mother shows her constant love not by constant admiration of her children, but by getting on with the next load of washing and the next meal. The leading of an act of worship, whether in choir or sanctuary, demands a degree of attention with the thing in hand which demands the whole of us. The very attention is part of the worship. So is the *in*tention. The mere fact of having been in church

139

one Sunday and taking it for granted that we shall be there the next, is in itself a character-forming thing.

One day God and the devil were watching a man saying his prayers. And because the lawn needed cutting, and he had had a bad day at the office, the man's thoughts were scattering all over the place. 'Just look at that,' the devil said to God, 'What's the use of that to you?' 'Don't be silly, devil,' said God, 'he isn't doing it to please you, and you can tell by his face he isn't doing it to please himself. But he is trying to please me, and badly though he is doing it, I accept his intention.' And you will be very fortunate indeed if you have no sympathy with the distracted mother's Saturday night prayer: 'Dear Lord, I shall be going to church tomorrow, and I know that by the time I have woken my husband up twice and washed and dressed the children and stopped the fight in the pew—I know that I shan't have much attention left for you. But my *intention* is to love and serve you, and that the children should grow up taking family worship for granted.'

Jesus knows all about distracted and irritable disciples. There was one occasion when the fishermen among them had slaved away all night with nothing to show for it, but who in simple obedience to him did the next thing. They did it reluctantly and grudgingly, but they did it. And they were almost overwhelmed by the catch of fish.

So we, in patient Christian service, with few rewards, fed-up, reluctant Christians as often as not—now and then, when we least deserve it, and when we least expect it, will respond to the Lord's command, 'Launch out into the deep!' And we shall be overwhelmed by our awareness of the living God.

PENTECOST 17

Religion without stain or fault

James 1.16–end (NEB)

1 *Gifts from above*

You have all been to meetings which have been interrupted by appeals to move a car, 'registration number so and so'. I am not giving numbers now, but if you have parked your car under the conker tree, probably at this very moment it is being rained upon by sticks and the remaining pieces of the vicarage fence. While one conker remains on that tree the abuse will go on. I usually do allow it to go on, on the principle that the more energy spent the shorter the season will be, though I do restrain fathers and older brothers, as having an unfair advantage. Whenever I appear on the battlefield there is a pause in the throwing, as boys stand poised for flight, but we usually come to some agreement about arms limitation.

I think that in law I, as vicar, have the rights of herbage in the churchyard, and this must surely mean not just the right to graze sheep, but that the conkers are mine! The thought of such wealth goes to my head. But like most of the best things in life they are an outright gift, and if you keep gifts to yourself something about them seems to spoil: 'The church which lives to itself dies by itself.' The principle of generosity is built into the Gospel: 'All good giving, every perfect gift, comes from above, from the Father of the lights of heaven.' Our new liturgy demonstrates that worship is not a closed circle, but a spring of mission.

We come to worship. 'The Lord is here', we shall be singing in a moment. 'The Lord is here, his Spirit is with us.' But our last words are, 'Go in peace to love and serve the Lord. In the name of Christ. Amen.' And that 'Amen' is not a sort of 'That's over and finished with' sort of Amen, not a 'Time now for egg and bacon. Amen', but a 'That is my resolve' sort of Amen. I will continue my worship by *using* what God has given me, in glorifying him in every part of my life, in bringing his gifts to the service of others.

2 *Be slow to speak*

Now one of God's great gifts to us is the gift of each other. And as you look around you, you might well think that is a funny thing to say. 'If she's a gift, then she's wrapped in a very odd sort of package.' But like a beautiful conker, the outside may well be unattractive and prickly. 'Away with the malice that hurries to excess,' says St James, and St Paul says 'Welcome each other without grumbling.'

It is very easy for any community, and this includes a Christian community, to be over-critical. People get tensed up, and everything becomes controversial, divisive. It is exhausting, because it absorbs a lot of spiritual energy which should be outgoing and fruitful. St Benedict was the great saint who framed a lot of rules for monasteries, and throughout his Rule he warns his monks against the vice of 'murmuring'. And another monk once said, 'Monks are like a herd of pigs—when one grunts they all grunt!' In one sense it is important to be critical, but not in the sense that when you find things are not to your liking this will upset you and cause you to grumble. There *is* a good constructive way of criticizing; but there is also a bad way, and that is what St Benedict was talking about. We learn from experience how easy it is to be destructively critical, to be over-hasty in making judgments, to be intolerant of the faults of others—their ignorance, short-sightedness, lack of vision.

3 *The law that makes us free*

The way out of this trap is through thanksgiving, looking in others for some goodness, some gift (for there is no one altogether without), and then to recognize that if there is any goodness, any gift, then it must come from God. And when you thank God for this gift you have sprung open the trap and love is free to grow. Nor need there be jealousy of others for their gifts, for each of us is unique. Just as no one else has the same finger-prints as you, no one has the same gifts, or the same opportunities for using them to the glory of God.

'A man may think he is religious, but if he has no control over his tongue, he is deceiving himself.' So welcome each other without grumbling. Each of us has received a special grace, so, like good stewards responsible for these different graces of God, let us put ourselves at the service of others. Go in peace, to love and serve the Lord.

PENTECOST 18

The generosity of God

2 Corinthians 8.1–9 (NEB)

1 *Rich in everything*

The parish presents an air of quiet prosperity and content, but we know that behind many a trim lawn and crisp net curtain there beats a heart weighed down with the mortgage. This is the generation of have-now-pay-later, whether we speak of property or things or human experience. So it is difficult to plead poverty while exuding such an air of prosperity.

The same problem afflicts the local church. The more care we lavish on our outward appearance, the more we struggle to keep up appearance, the more bravely we smile as the bills come in, the less sympathy we receive.

'The Church is wealthy,' people say. And who can deny it? We have the treasury of God to draw on, we wear fine clothing, we live in kings' houses. But that is not the same as ready cash. The millions which the Church Commissioners administer (which, in spite of the man in the train, are not knowingly derived from sweated labour or the rents of prostitutes)—these millions are spread very thinly indeed, as they help to maintain just a small part of the full-time ministry of the Church. And it dies very hard—the idea that the Church is some kind of adjunct to the Welfare State.

Now the truth is, that apart from one sixth of me which is paid for by those who lie outside in long low graves, this whole apparatus of church and plant and staff would grind to a halt without the income we pour into it. This is part of our ministry, not only to God, but to the community in which we live. There are priests to marry the lovers and to bury the dead and to forgive the penitent, *only* because *we* pay for them. Church schools and priests to teach in them are here—only because we pay for them. Englishmen, bolstered by rich patrons, have always had their religion on the cheap. This is the first generation when there is growing a direct relation between the man in the pew and what actually is done. Alleluia!

2 *Stewardship in Macedonia*

Now, without exactly expecting you to stand up and cheer, I hope I have carried you with me so far. But paying for what we get is only common honesty, not Christian stewardship; getting only what we pay for only commonsense, not the gospel of the love of Christ.

For we must start at the other end of the story:

As Christians we hold, as treasure for the world, the truth that we have been created not out of some inner necessity on the part of God, but out of the sheer bounty of his love. We have been not only created in love but redeemed, at a cost of love so great that we can never understand, but only worship and adore. We have been not only created and redeemed, but promised infinite joy.

> *We must tell you, friends, about the grace of generosity which God has imparted to our congregations in Macedonia. The troubles they have been through have tried them hard, yet in all this they have been so exuberantly happy that from the depths of*

144

their poverty they have shown themselves lavishly open-handed.

Nothing that we are or that we have is our own, except our sin, and our freedom to love God in return. And after his gift to us of freewill, his greatest gift to us is his trust, to use his creation to his glory.

3 *Stewardship at home*

The Christian even remotely aware of his stewardship never says, 'This for me, this for Mabel, this for God.' His prudent care of Mabel and the children is part of his love for God; his gift to the Church is an inevitable sign of his love for God, and his mutual trust in all others who love God.

My time (as we like so strangely to call it), my abilities (as we like so proudly to claim them), my wealth—all is God's and merely entrusted to me. And on my stewardship of that trust I am already judged.

> *By telling you how keen others are I am putting your love to the test. For you know how generous our Lord Jesus Christ has been: he was rich, yet for your sake he became poor, so that through his poverty you might become rich.*

King David wished to worship God, and he sought from Araunah the Jebusite a part of his ground, his threshing-floor, on which to build an altar. And, because David was the king, Araunah would gladly have given it to him. But with an exquisite sense of stewardship, and combining in one breath the responsibility of wealth and worship and sacrifice, the king insisted on paying for it, and said, 'I will not offer to the Lord that which costs me nothing'.

PENTECOST 19

Faith gives substance to our hopes

Hebrews 11.1–2, 8–16 (NEB)

1 *One as good as dead*

All the little boys called 'Falkland' will soon be old enough to regret it. It's funny how we are shy about our own names. They are so much a part of us that telling them lowers our defences. But the 'Falklands' and 'Jubilees' are nothing new. There is a tradition as old as mankind of names having meanings. One of my favourites is the name once given to a boy in the Old Testament. He was called 'Ichabod'. Let me tell you about him.

His mother was the daughter-in-law of the prophet Samuel, though you don't have to remember that. But just as she was about to have this poor child news came through that the Philistines had defeated the Israelites and captured the Ark of God, the sign of God's presence at the heart of Israel. The women who stood by her said, 'Do not be afraid, you have given birth to a son.' But she took no notice. She named the boy 'Ichabod', meaning 'The glory has departed'—the glory has departed because the Ark of God has been captured.

Ichabod', poor child! She was talking utter nonsense, of course, though perhaps a woman in her circumstances may be excused for doing so. Far from the glory having departed there was to follow the whole majesty of the Kingdom of David, the great prophets, and the gradual hallowing of the nation to receive Jesus himself. What to human eyes was glory departing was to God another opportunity of manifesting his glory.

2 *There sprang descendants*

Indeed, looking back, and being wise after the event, it was not until Israel had lost the Ark, and ceased to imagine that they could carry God about in a box, that they could respond more fully to their vocation as the people of God. We remember the Psalmist's profound wisdom: 'It is good for me to have been in trouble, that I might learn thy statutes,' and again, 'Thou of very faithfulness hast caused me to be troubled'.

There are many in our generation prepared to cry 'Ichabod'—the glory has departed; and if the truth be known most of us have a bit of him in our constitution. We hanker for what has been. We feel vulnerable at the loss of assurances and familiar ways of doing things. But the God whom we worship is the living God, infinitely greater, infinitely more holy, infinitely more wonderful than we can ever imagine. Our relationship with him is not a static one, one that stands still. Even in our relationships with one another that is not true: how much less true with God! His will for us, his purpose, is always unfolding, revealing new wonders and new depths of his love. The pangs we suffer are birth pangs, and the outcome is more life, more joy, more hope. 'Thou of very faithfulness hast caused me to be troubled.'

3 *A city ready for them*

The Chinese have a proverb that 'the longest journey begins with one step'.

> *All these persons died in faith. They were not yet in possession of the things promised, but had seen them far ahead and hailed them, and confessed themselves no more than strangers or passing travellers on earth.*

There is not one person here who has not a next step to take in his adventure with God. It may be a prayer, a confession, being confirmed. God will show you, given half the chance. No longer 'Ichabod' but the writing of his new name upon your heart, and the dawning of glory new.

There is no parish which does not have a next step to take in its adventure with God. No longer 'Ichabod' but new vocation, fresh service, further vision. Our God is not the God of the dead but of the living.

> *We find them longing for a better country—I mean, the heavenly one. That is why God is not ashamed to be called their God; for he has a city ready for them.*

PENTECOST 20

Endurance

> *Romans 8.18–25 (RSV)*

1 *Patience*

During the last war, among the exhortations to 'Dig For Victory', and warnings that 'Walls have Ears', there was a series of posters which featured a little character called Percy. Do you remember Percy? He was the child of Mr and Mrs Vere. And Percy Vere was held up to us as an example of the man who got on with things, who didn't give up.

The Alternative Service Book has not actually put Percy Vere into the Calendar, but it has provided for this Sunday the theme of 'Endurance'. And the readings chosen for today all illustrate this quality: Shadrach, Meshach and Abed-nego in the burning fiery furnace; St Paul with his 'Hope' ('We hope for what we do not see, we wait for it with patience'); and the warning of Jesus, 'No one who sets his hand to the plough, and then keeps looking back, is fit for the kingdom of God'.

Percy-verence is not an easy quality to commend, but it is revealing to note that 'patience' is very much a New Testament word. It does not seem to occur in the Old Testament at all—it is very much a Christian attribute. Perhaps because it did not come naturally to him, St Paul is always urging the necessity of patience. And with Jesus there was a kind of divine imperative which drove him on, a holy *im*-patience to fulfil his Father's will. 'O stupid and *slow* of heart to believe!' But as Gregory Dix points out, this impatience was but a tendency to be swift and to see clearly and move directly to his goal, and was always balanced in his life with a sort of meticulous waiting upon the will of God.

Christian patience is surely more than not stamping one's foot if the train is late. It is a steadfastness, a stability.

2 *Stability*

Now there's a good word: Stability!

We know how monks and nuns are bound to their religious rules by vows, and traditionally we think of these vows as threefold—of chastity, poverty and obedience—three ways in which they are set free, to be free for God. But in the Benedictine tradition, that balance of worship, work and recreation which has so influenced our own Anglican heritage, in the Benedictine community monks make one vow only. It is the vow of 'stability', the promise to remain within the community, a putting of the hand to the plough and not looking back.

I am sure that when we get to heaven we shall discover what we owe to those among us who possess to a very deep degree this gift of stability. If we don't notice them so much now it is because they are always there, taken for granted, quietly faithful to their Church, faithful to their family, faithful to their friends.

We are greatly mistaken if we confuse this Christian stability with weak acquiescence or lack of spirit. It has to be fought for, every inch of the way. In these people there is great strength below the surface. And we are greatly mistaken if we confuse it with stubbornness, the Cornish 'not belonging' to do new things, for it is a commitment to God within a community, and as the community grows and changes so will they. But they will always be there. They have put their hands to the plough and will not look back.

3 *Hope*

St Paul puts his finger on the secret when he mentions the word 'hope'. Hope is one of the great virtues, in which we are meant to grow. In a stained glass window of 'faith, hope and charity', hope is usually the rather wan looking lady on the left, obviously expecting the worst to happen. Whereas in real honest Christian life the hopeful person will be the practical one getting on with the next thing. For Christian hope is not a longing that things might be other than they are. It is the certainty that affairs are safe in the hands of God, in the words of the Lady Julian that 'all things are well, and all manner of things shall be well.' It is Christian assurance.

It is easy to test the presence of hope by noting its opposites, presumption and despair. Presumption is cocksureness. And we are all guilty of this when we trivialize God, when we are unaware of his greatness and majesty and holiness. The casual communicant is a person without the virtue of hope, for he is oblivious of God. And when we despair, of ourselves or of God, it is due to a lack of hope, a failure to believe the promises of God.

It is the certainty of God which is the source of our endurance. And this is true equally of the dramatic cry of a George Tyrrell, 'How often would I have thrown the whole thing up, but always that strange young man on his cross drives me back again,' and of the undramatic little old lady who knows that life is a pretty rough affair, but does not allow this for one minute to diminish her trust in God.

True hope is possible only if the ultimates in life give ground for hope. And the grounds of Christian hope are God's eternity and Christ's resurrection, and also God's goodness—that he will not abandon us for whom Christ lived and died. Such confidence is a gift of the Holy Spirit. Nor is it merely being confident that our own eternal destiny is in good hands. God has good things in store for all men:

I consider that the sufferings of this present time are not worth comparing with the glory that is to be revealed to us. For the creation waits with eager longing . . . .

Many years ago, when I was a student under the care of the Community of the Resurrection, it was the wisdom of the Mirfield Fathers to place among us one or two of their older brethren. It meant that in a rather youthful and exuberant household there were at least some members who needed care and patience. Of course, when the deaf were listened to, we were rewarded with their wisdom and humour. I have often quoted this as an illustration of the need for courtesy and patience. But I realize now that what I gained from these elders in the faith was not just a lesson in good manners, but a remarkable example of stability, of patience, of endurance. Not a grim hanging-on, but a joyful pilgrimage, with a gleam in their eye as they entered the home straight.

There are some of you like that, and we thank God for you.

PENTECOST 21

Our customs and disputes

Acts 26.1–8 (NEB)

1 *Permission to speak for yourself*

We forget how recently it was that the man in the pew was given a voice in the management of Church affairs. It was out of the First World War that there came a great movement for reform—the Life and Liberty Movement. And if to us the existence of a parochial church council does not immediately inspire thoughts of life and liberty, we must recognize what a revolution its existence represents.

The first two minute books of the PCC rest upon my shelves, and I often dip into them with a mixture of nostalgia and amusement. Some of you can remember the rather formidable vicar who chaired those first meetings, and it is fascinating to see the familiar family names appear. 'It was asked why the Amen after the ascription was not sung. The vicar explained the difficulty with visiting preachers, and of the organist having to regain his seat in a hurry.' Here is a nice slice of annual meeting business: 'The vicar explained that the parish was entitled, according to scale, to elect ten representatives. Mr Vos thought *six* would be quite enough, and Miss Debenham *eight*. Finally the following *nine* were elected.'

2 *A hope kindled by God's promise*

But it would be a gross misrepresentation to suggest that these petty matters were the whole of their concern. Through the records and memories we have glimpses of the people of God deeply concerned, not just with self-preservation, but with the extension of Christ's kingdom in the parish, and throughout the world. We see the idea of a parish mission taking shape; we note the prophet voices never letting the council forget the needy and deprived people of the world; we sense faithful ministry and loving concern.

The first effect of a growing sense of history, which develops, they say, with increasing age, is a very humbling one. It reduces us to scale. We are not the first to be here, nor shall we be the last.

The second effect is one of encouragement as we come to realize that there never was an ideal time (except in our highly selective imaginations) when all was well, and which we must struggle to retain or return to. As Adam said to Eve, 'We live in an age of transition!' We are always at the point of decision. We are always seeking the firm ground on which to place our next step.

152

3 *With intense devotion day and night*

What I am trying to commend is the very Christian concern for the present moment—the 'doctrine of NOW'. You cannot change the past; you do not know the future; the only moment in time you can immediately affect is the present moment. It is no good saying that we loved God once upon a time, or that we shall love God at some point in the future—like St Augustine, who prayed, 'Lord, make me chaste, but not yet!' It is the love and obedience of our hearts at this present moment, and every present moment, that God wants. Given that, he will take care of the next step. 'Set your hearts on his kingdom first, and on his righteousness . . . do not worry about tomorrow: tomorrow will take care of itself. Each day has enough trouble of its own.'

It is worth pushing this point a bit. To imagine that we can return to the past—any past—is going to bring us a lot of unhappiness. But we do need to be assured that nothing done for God is ever wasted. Lives of faithfulness and obedience given to God, even if fashions in faithfulness and obedience may appear to have changed, are never wasted. Within the providence of God all times are present to him—all present moments—and the obedience and love we have shown at each of those moments are precious to him.

But if we need to be rescued from slavery to the past, we need release also from the tyranny of the future. It is the essence of the Marxist philosophy that it transfers the ideal world from the past to the future. To put it over-simply, but graphically, instead of a garden of Eden in the past we have a utopia in the future. But you see what I mean about the tyranny of the future: in reaching this utopia the people of any particular generation become means to an end. Their happiness and prosperity, and their very lives, can be sacrificed for the imaginery benefit of the distant view. Man has no value except as a means to an imaginary end—there is enough evidence of this in the world today.

153

Over against the hankering for the past and the hankering for the future, the Christian remains the true realist, taking every breath as a present gift from God, loving the present moment because this is his opportunity to opt for God and the things of God (over against all that clamours for his attention and distraction) grateful for the good things of the past, but free—free to move with the wind of the Spirit, who blows where *he* wills.

'Keep thou my feet, I do not ask to see the distant scene! one step enough for me.'

PENTECOST 22

What you were taught in the beginning

1 John 2.22–end (JB)

1 *He is the liar*

On Whit Monday the Archbishop of Canterbury went to our Lady's shrine at Walsingham, as did some people from this parish, and about fifteen thousand others. There were also present a few protesters, as there always are on Whit Monday, whether the Archbishop is there or not. By waiting across the road from them, photographers were able to get a picture of the Archbishop framed against their banners, and this was the news item served up to the nation.

There are always two questions we should have in our minds when we look at the papers—not only, 'Is this true?', but, 'What is its context?'. Because it is the selection of news which can twist the truth. In this instance a few protesters, as so often, were the news, the Archbishop came next, and our dear Mother Mary, for whom fifteen thousand were thanking God, came third. In the same sort of way, with the Passion Play at Oberammergau, it is the differences of opinion about the Jewishness or anti-Jewishness of the text which makes the headlines, and into the background fade the drama that is presented and the vow faithfully kept.

If we Christians can detect the false emphasis in these things we happen to know about, it is our duty to subject all we are presented with to the same critical analysis—'Is this true?' 'Is this the whole truth?' And if a malicious piece of gossip turns out not to be true, are we glad, or are we secretly rather sorry?

2 *In shame at his coming*

Nevertheless, Christians have a remarkable capacity for washing their dirty linen in public, and, although we needn't fool ourselves that if we presented a united front people would flock to Christ, there is not the slightest doubt that arguments and divisions within the Church cause others to stumble. 'To cause to stumble' is what 'scandalize' actually means.

Here it might be worthwhile having another look at the old distinction between 'unity' and 'uniformity'. Because if anything new is growing in this matter it is a growing thankfulness to God for our diversity—seeing the different ways of worship and the variety of Christian experience not dividing the faith but enriching it. On the world stage the discussions between Roman Catholics and the Eastern Orthodox Churches have got off to a new start because written into the agenda is thanksgiving for diversity. So here in this parish I am glad we have a bit of a 'mixed economy', where our different styles, far from antagonizing, are seen to enrich us. No, it is not uniformity we want—everyone being the same. But where do we find our unity?

3 *Live in Christ*

We read of the first Christians that 'they remained faithful to the teaching of the apostles, to the fellowship, to the breaking of bread, and the prayers'. Wherever we find these four 'marks' of the Church, there we are at home. If we want to test the value of Christian experience this is the test we apply: does it come within these character-istics? They are like the family likeness which runs through any family, likeness or not just of feature but of manner and even mannerism.

Where we find these four characteristics we find authentic Christian experience. First, 'the teaching of the apostles'. This can be reduced to two statements: 'We saw Jesus killed, we know him to be alive.' The Church is the community of the Resurrection, and in any authentic Christian community there will be an awareness of Jesus as Lord, a living person who holds us in his heart and mind. Second, 'the fellowship'. There can be no such thing as an isolated Christian. You can't be a Christian without being part of a Church, because the gifts of God are given in community. Third, 'the breaking of bread'. The frequency and style of the sacrament may vary, but of its centrality there must be no question. You can have an altar without a church building, but no church is a church without the Lord's table. Then 'the prayers'—that aware-ness of worshipping in a stream of adoration bigger than the individual, larger than the congregation.

We have spoken of family likeness. Without losing that insight, let us also think in terms of friendship. Because the great thing about friends is that they discover each other, and they find themselves saying or thinking, 'So you see things that way too!' The same things appear good, and the same things appear ridiculous. Friends weep at the same things and laugh at the same things, and together are moved to silence.

So when Christians of different traditions discover each other they say, 'So that is how you are moved,' 'So that is how you feel,' and, above all, 'We have a friend in common—if Jesus is your friend, you are a friend of mine'. God is so great that although we are all made in his image and grow in his likeness, we can be gloriously different from each other. It is not surprising that these differences make us react in different ways, but this is a matter not for grief, but of thanksgiving.

It has been pointed out that the characteristic posture

of lovers is to face each other, excluding the world. But friends walk side by side, facing in the same direction, and presenting to the world (if they are Christian friends) the face of Christ.

LAST SUNDAY AFTER PENTECOST

Our Homeland is in Heaven

> *Philippians 3.7–end (JB)*

1 *Eternal dimension*

A generation ago there died one of the very great churchmen of this century, Milner White. Even if the name seems unfamiliar to you, he has probably influenced you considerably through the prayers he wrote to embellish the old liturgy.

Milner White was successively Dean of King's College, Cambridge and Dean of York, and therefore spent most of his life with two of the most beautiful churches there are. There is an apocryphal tale that when he reached Paradise he looked round with a rather critical eye and began to suggest improvements.

At the end of a long ministry he told how he had been engaged in three particular battles: one to restore the Blessed Sacrament to the centre of Anglican worship; one to see the sacrament of forgiveness accepted as a normal thing. Before telling you of the third, I invite you to take a sideways look at the victories he marked, and wonder if his preoccupations would have been the same today, concerned as we are with ministry and authority and unity. I mention this because it is moving demonstration of the way the Holy Spirit gives to the Church certain concerns and anxieties in each generation. Just as the luxuries of one generation become the necessities of the next, so do old battles seem very remote indeed, and victories become assumptions.

But back to his third battle. He regarded this as yet to be won, and I would suggest that it still needs to be fought today. We need, he said, 'to recover the sense of the eternal'.

Now what did he mean by that? I take him to have meant the awareness that our life is lived against the background of heaven. Not simply that we shall eventually come to heaven, but that God reigns now outside our human limitations of time and space, and we are already—now—the citizens of two worlds. This is an awareness that the Eastern Orthodox Church has never lost, and will therefore be its particular contribution to a united Christendom. An old Hertfordshire countryman once described the saintly Bishop Loyd of St Albans as having a 'yon-type' religion. I think we know what he meant.

Christians, of course, must not be so heavenly minded that they are no earthly good, but isn't it true that the Christians who have in fact done the most earthly good have been exactly those who have had this other dimension in their lives, who know Jesus not as a dead hero, but as a living Lord, who live in conscious fellowship with the saints, in whose company we laud and magnify God's Holy Name?

If that sounds a bit high-falutin, let us come down to earth—literally. In the nature of things I go to more funerals than you do, and spend more time with the bereaved. And there is all the difference in the world between a funeral when death is thought of as the end, and one where through all the unhappiness and distress there is the awareness of this other dimension, of life with a purpose and a destiny. You can't in five minutes drum up this awareness; it is the fruit of a life-long attitude.

2 *Home with mother*

We celebrate the honour which is due uniquely to the Blessed Virgin Mary, since (to quote the hymn) next to his throne her Son his Mother placed. And if I have come

158

rather a long way round to get there it is because I wanted to demonstrate how fruitless it is to discuss the deep and holy mystery of Mary's place in our redemption without this awareness of heaven. To some people devotion to Mary is irrelevant. Others go to the opposite extreme and allow her to usurp divinity, and this leads to superstition. Both these states are the result of a failure to appreciate the reality of eternal life, and a failure to appreciate the greatness of God. 'My soul doth magnify the Lord,' is Mary's song. It was her song on earth, and it remains her song in heaven. And where our love of her is true she magnifies—she makes greater—our vision of God.

I don't know that 'Assumption' is the happiest title to have given to this joyful truth. It is not a title I would have chosen, however accurate the technical root from which it comes, but then I wasn't consulted! It is a Latin characteristic to over-define everything; whereas it is a more homely British characteristic to stumble along a bit and make do. You notice how this is reflected in the different attitudes to law: Roman law is codified and precise; English case law gets there in the end, but is based on commonsense reaction to situations presented to us. So faced with the wonder of Mary's fulfilment in triumph in heaven, the Roman mind goes into great detail of how she got there. The English attitude is better reflected in the following story. The Sunday School teacher asked her class, 'And who wants to go to heaven?' All the children put up their hands (sycophantic little beasts) except one. 'Don't you want to go to heaven?' he was asked. 'No,' he sobbed, 'my mum says I've got to go straight home!'

Christians live day by day in the knowledge that within the loving purpose of God, heaven is their home. And if heaven is our home, what more natural place could there be in which to find our Mother?

3 *Because of Christ*

It is the hope of heaven which gives us perspective in this

world, and which shows the things of this world in their true values. So St Paul can write to the Philippians:

I look on everything as so much rubbish if only I can have Christ and be given a place in him . . . for us our homeland is in heaven, and from heaven comes the saviour we are waiting for, the Lord Jesus Christ, and he will transfigure these wretched bodies of ours into copies of his glorious body. He will do that by the same power with which he can subdue the whole universe.

And today the Church prays:

Merciful God,
you have prepared for those who love you
such good things as pass man's understanding.
Pour into our hearts such love towards you
that we, loving you above all things,
may obtain your promises,
which exceed all that we can desire;
through Jesus Christ our Lord.

Other Mowbray Sermon Outlines

Series Editor: D. W. Cleverley Ford

Preaching at the Parish Communion ASB Lectionary
Gospels—Sundays: Year One by Dennis Runcorn
Gospels—Sundays: Year Two by Raymond Wilkinson

Preaching through the Christian Year
Vol. 7 by Alan Dunstan
Vol. 8 by Frank Colquhoun
Vol. 9 by Robert Martineau

Preaching on Special Occasions Volume Two
by D. W. Cleverley Ford

More Preaching from the New Testament
by D. W. Cleverley Ford

More Preaching from the Old Testament
by D. W. Cleverley Ford

Preaching through the Acts of the Apostles
by D. W. Cleverley Ford

Preaching through the Prophets
by John B. Taylor

Preaching through the Psalms
by D. W. Cleverley Ford

Preaching through Saint Paul
by Derrick Greeves